Tropical Plant Design
20 Difficult Situations

How to Use the 10 Best Commercially-Hardy Plants

David L. Hamilton

TROPICAL PLANT DESIGN
20 Difficult Situations
David L. Hamilton

1999 Excerpt from Hamilton's Commercial Indoor Plants
Original Printing 1985

Park Place Publications
P.O. Box 829
Pacific Grove, CA 93950
Telephone (831) 649-6640
Toll free (888) 702-4500

ORDER BOOKS ONLINE
www.parkplace-publications.com

© Copyright 1999 by Patricia Hamilton
All rights reserved. Printed in U.S.A.

PRINTED IN THE U.S.A.

ISBN 1-877809-65-9

Tropical Plant Design
20 Difficult Situations

How to Use the 10 Best Commercially-Hardy Plants

David L. Hamilton

PARK PLACE PUBLICATIONS

The 20 Difficult Design Situations using

PLANTS FOR EXTREMELY LOW LIGHT   8
  Characteristics of low light plants
  Water requirements in 5 to 30 footcandles
  Rootbound plants dry out faster
  Watering technique for low light
THE 10 BEST LOW LIGHT PLANTS

LONG LASTING HANGING PLANTS   10
  Characteristics of hardy hanging plants
  Stresses on the roots caused by the foliage weight
  Light gathering abilities of large thick leaves
  Hanging plants require extra maintenance
THE 10 MOST DURABLE HANGING PLANTS

HARDY, LOW LIGHT FLOWERING PLANTS   12
  Lighting accumulations for flowering plants
  Porous soil and constricted roots
  Feeding schedules and seasonal lighting
  Extending the blossoming period
THE 10 HARDIEST FLOWERING PLANTS

TALL, NARROW, UPRIGHT PLANTS   14
  Problems with a wide plant in a narrow space
  Shaping a Palm to fit against a wall
  Trimming back the excess foliage
  Shape control is easiest during the first few days
10 SUITABLE FORMS FOR TIGHT CORNERS

DURABLE GROUNDCOVERS AND TRAILING VINES   16
  The difficulty with planted-out groundcovers
  Methods for keeping them in their original pots
  Companion plantings
  The difference between trailers and fillers
10 STRONG, MULTI-PURPOSE VINES

DARK, RICH-GREEN LEAVES   18
  Dark green leaves look healthy
  They contrast to muted colors
  Feeding deepens the foliage color
  Organic plant food is safe and effective
10 FLOOR PLANTS WITH DEEP GREEN LEAVES

LARGE, EXOTIC AND DRAMATIC LEAF FORMS   20
  Indoor leaves grow larger because of reduced light
  They also become thinner
  Plants gradually alter their whole form
  Selective pruning and long term growth
10 LARGE, ELABORATE LEAF STRUCTURES

EXCITING, MULTI-COLORED LEAVES   22
  The availability of various color combinations
  Green and cream are the most common
  Tricolored plants
  Using glazed planters with variegated foliage
10 BRIGHTLY-COLORED TROPICAL PLANTS

DELICATE, FEATHERY FOLIAGE PATTERNS   24
  Delicate foliage often needs humidity
  Finely textured leaves suit window lighting
  Some plants look more delicate from a distance
  Architectural possibilities with small leaves
10 EXAMPLES OF LIGHT, AIRY FOLIAGE

PLANTS WITH ATTRACTIVE STEMS AND TRUNKS   26
  Plants with larger stems need more light
  Removing some foliage liberates the stem
  Loose bark indicates poor health
  Shrinking stems foretell eventual failure
10 LARGE TROPICALS WITH OUTSTANDING STEMS

the 10 Best Commercially-Hardy Plants

PLANTS FOR EXTREMELY LOW LIGHT — 28
  Characteristics of low light plants
  Water requirements in 5 to 30 footcandles
  Rootbound plants dry out faster
  Watering technique for low light
THE 10 BEST LOW LIGHT PLANTS

LONG LASTING HANGING PLANTS — 30
  Characteristics of hardy hanging plants
  Stresses on the roots caused by the foliage weight
  Light gathering abilities of large thick leaves
  Hanging plants require extra maintenance
THE 10 MOST DURABLE HANGING PLANTS

HARDY, LOW LIGHT FLOWERING PLANTS — 32
  Lighting accumulations for flowering plants
  Porous soil and constricted roots
  Feeding schedules and seasonal lighting
  Extending the blossoming period
THE 10 HARDIEST FLOWERING PLANTS

TALL, NARROW, UPRIGHT PLANTS — 34
  Problems with a wide plant in a narrow space
  Shaping a Palm to fit against a wall
  Trimming back the excess foliage
  Shape control is easiest during the first few days
10 SUITABLE FORMS FOR TIGHT CORNERS

DURABLE GROUNDCOVERS AND TRAILING VINES — 36
  The difficulty with planted-out groundcovers
  Methods for keeping them in their original pots
  Companion plantings
  The difference between trailers and fillers
10 STRONG, MULTI-PURPOSE VINES

DARK, RICH-GREEN LEAVES — 38
  Dark green leaves look healthy
  They contrast to muted colors
  Feeding deepens the foliage color
  Organic plant food is safe and effective
10 FLOOR PLANTS WITH DEEP GREEN LEAVES

LARGE, EXOTIC AND DRAMATIC LEAF FORMS — 40
  Indoor leaves grow larger because of reduced light
  They also become thinner
  Plants gradually alter their whole form
  Selective pruning and long term growth
10 LARGE, ELABORATE LEAF STRUCTURES

EXCITING, MULTI-COLORED LEAVES — 42
  The availability of various color combinations
  Green and cream are the most common
  Tricolored plants
  Using glazed planters with variegated foliage
10 BRIGHTLY-COLORED TROPICAL PLANTS

DELICATE, FEATHERY FOLIAGE PATTERNS — 44
  Delicate foliage often needs humidity
  Finely textured leaves suit window lighting
  Some plants look more delicate from a distance
  Architectural possibilities with small leaves
10 EXAMPLES OF LIGHT, AIRY FOLIAGE

PLANTS WITH ATTRACTIVE STEMS AND TRUNKS — 46
  Plants with larger stems need more light
  Removing some foliage liberates the stem
  Loose bark indicates poor health
  Shrinking stems foretell eventual failure
10 LARGE TROPICALS WITH OUTSTANDING STEMS

Botanical Name Index — 48

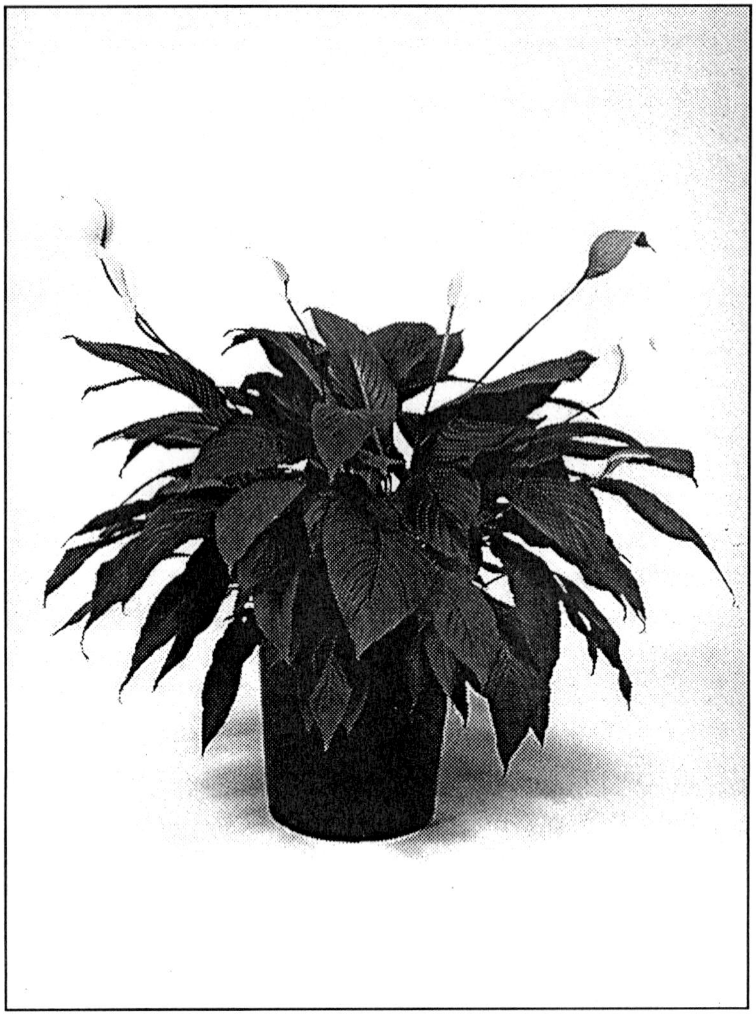

Designing in Difficult Situations

Difficult environmental situations can be a playground for the designer. This is the one arena where overachieving is sure to bring rave reviews from all other plant professionals. The client may not know how hard it was to make a plant grow in a particular spot (they often think all plants grow everywhere), but compliments from one's peers are a treasure to cherish. And while the conditions listed in this chapter encompass the standard litany for problems, there is a further challenge that grows from using other than sure-fire winners in demanding places.

Today's body of knowledge on indoor plants has only been collected because people have tried to use plants in many different circumstances. However, the list of potential uses can be expanded. Sometimes, the conditions can be modified. Spotlighting is an obvious solution to light problems, but automatic misting to increase the humidity, and methods for warming up the coldness of a root mass are others.

One reason plants grow better in the nursery is the higher soil temperatures. Raising the indoor soil temperature from 65°F to 80°F will create a plant that accepts 30% less light. Soil temperature can be increased through the use of insulating mulches, porous soil, warm watering water, and—if the client accepts the expense—by electrical means.

Occasionally, tropical plants are the key element to the decor, and any reasonable cost is appropriate. Large planters are easily warmed when lighting is installed beneath the bottom of the pot —and the light will illuminate the surrounding floor spaces as an added benefit. This procedure additionally dries out the bottom roots—which are the ones needing the most help.

By combining warm roots, humidity and spotlighting together, the designer may be able to place just about any plant in the darkest of corners. For experimental purposes, try using a heating pad beneath the planter of a foliage plant in a poorly-lit space. Within 4 weeks, the plant will put on a spurt of fresh new growth.

Plants for Extremely Low Light

Characteristics of low light plants.

Low light is the most difficult interior situation for plants. Their ability to survive depends on a complex interaction, including slow growth, water storage in the roots, a low transpiration rate, and the ability to gather light efficiently. The plants in this group do not come from the forest floor—even though the natural light is low there. They come from dry tropical areas, where the premium is on thick leaves and low water demands. Plants from the dark forest floor are accustomed to high humidity, and high humidity is normally equated with bright indoor lighting.

Water requirements in 5 to 30 footcandles.

In low light, plants grow slowly, and when they grow slowly, they use water at less than 1/10 the rate of a window plant. In fact, as much water may exit the root mass through evaporation, as is used by the plant itself. In the range of 5 and 30 footcandles, even the hardiest plants will need water only every 2-4 weeks, and some need moisture only every 2 or 3 months.

Rootbound plants dry out faster.

Since wet roots are the major cause of plant failures, low light watering is a delicate operation. Fortunately, there are 2 things that can weight the odds in the plant's favor. The first, and most important, is the ratio of roots to soil. When a plant is rootbound (over 80% roots to soil), it has the ability to gather soil moisture wherever it is in the pot. This prevents root failure caused by pockets of soil that stay damp and cold. The best low light plants take the moisture available after watering, and quickly store it in the roots, stems and foliage. Then, the plant can make its own decision on how fast to use it, without worrying about 'wet feet'.

Watering technique for low light.

The second key to success involves drying time and the method for pouring the water. The soil must be dried until the plant starts to wilt, then the water is added slowly and sparingly—so that all the roots are barely moistened. This way they dry out the fastest.

THE 10 BEST LOW LIGHT PLANTS

1. **Corn Plants**
   Dracaenas

   For size, beauty and durability, this family is clearly number one for extreme low light conditions. Fragrans is the hardiest, followed by Janet Craig and Warneckei. The bush form of Fragrans tolerates 25 fc indefinitely, while the cane form needs 30 fc. Corn Plants over 10' tall require slightly more light.

2. **Cast Iron Plant**
   Aspidistra eliator

   Typical of leather-leafed Lilies, the Aspidistra grows so slowly it can survive 10 fc for at least 1 year—providing it is watered every 2 or 3 months. The variegated form features randomly colored, variable width stripes. The strongest plants have 20-30 leaves in a 10 inch pot.

3. **Bamboo Palms**
   Chamaedoreas

   The dwarf, Neanthe Bella, is capable of living comfortably in 20 fc. Erumpens needs 30 fc. Both plants become gracefully angular after 1 year in low light. After the Erumpens reaches 12', the canes become too weak to support the foliage. Neanthe Bella stops growing taller at 4 to 5 feet.

4. **Snake Plant**
   Sansevieria species

   Some varieties may reach 4', others form low growing rosettes. All well rooted varieties can live in 5 fc for 6-12 months. They rarely need water. Colorations are endless, ranging from deep blue-greens through yellow-greens, to rich cream and pure white. 20 fc is plenty of light for all varieties.

5. **Lady Palm**
   Rhapis excelsa

   For its size and bushiness, this is an astounding palm. The serrated, finger-shaped fronds can take 30 fc and still hold themselves erect. Large specimens over 10' may require 45 fc, but even in low light, suckers will spring from the roots—and the plant continuously gets thicker and fuller.

6. **Marginata**
   Dracaena marginata

   Even though not quite as low light tolerant as some other family members, the Marginata becomes the most graceful. While shedding its stiff nursery leaves, the new growth begins to arch downward, changing the plant's shape more radically than any other indoor plant. The change takes 6-24 months.

7. **Chinese Evergreen**
   Aglaonema species

   While nearly like the Dieffenbachia in appearance, this plant is 3 times as hardy. It grows slowly, stays bushy, and the foliage rarely burns from low light. 35 fc is sufficient for long term survival. Many varieties are brightly variegated. Maximum height is 4 to 6 feet.

8. **Hardy Vines**
   Philodendron types

   Most Philodendrons are good low light plants—the Cordatum is best. **Epipremnum aureum** (Pothos) is even better, and **Syngonium podophyllum** (Nephthytis) tops them all. At 25 fc, growth is leggy, but over 40 fc all hardy Vines grow lush and full. Pruning encourages basal growth.

9. **Leather Fern**
   Rumohra adiantiformis

   No other fern even comes close to the Leather Fern in ability to grow in light below 30 fc. The stiff 'carrot top' fronds grow from creeping surface rhizomes. Mature plants exceed 3' in diameter. The rhizomes spill over the edge of the pot, or climb upward when supports are available.

10. **Barrel Cactus**
    Ferocactus

    Cacti love full sun, but their efficient water storage capacity makes them suitable for extended periods (6 months to 2 years) in less than 30 fc. Mature 3' Barrel Cacti do not change perceptably, even after 2 years in low light without being watered.

Long Lasting Hanging Plants

*Characteristics
of hardy hanging plants.*

Hanging plants have the reputation for being the least durable tropicals. They have acquired this stigma because generally they require a lot of light, and also, their vines are often semi-succulent and break off easily. All Vines are more at home in a planter bed, however, the plants on the facing page have strong stems, long lasting leaves, and tolerate reduced light.

*Stresses on the roots
caused by
the foliage weight.*

A hanging plant becomes pendant because the vines collapse over the edge of the pot under the weight of the foliage. This puts undue stress on the roots—to anchor the vines in the soil. Many hanging plant failures result as much from disturbed roots as from miswatering. As the root mass dries out between waterings, it 'opens up', and the vines slowly tug the roots out of the soil.

Hanging plants must be securely rooted to have success indoors. In addition, they need a stem with enough internal strength to stand the pulling weight of the foliage. The third ingredient to success is the light gathering ability of the leaves.

*Light gathering abilities
of large thick leaves.*

Most of the hardiest types have large thick leaves, and they are good low light candidates. Others have papery thin leaves, like the Fig Tree, and while they need more light, they are still efficient gatherers.

All hanging plants, even the long lived ones, require a high intensity of maintenance. Since they grow relatively faster than floor plants, there is always some trimming required with each maintenance visit. Also, their containers are harder to water and often are hung in impossible places.

*Hanging plants require
extra maintenance.*

When the designer is specifying hanging plants other than those listed here, replacement and maintenance costs may be 3 to 5 times as great. Maintenance personnel fear hanging plants, and rate them in the same category as visits to the dentist. The designer can help by making the plants accessible, and using them only as a last resort.

THE 10 MOST DURABLE HANGING PLANTS

1. **Nephthytis**
   Syngonium podophyllum

   This plant grows a large root mass for a Vine. The stems are quite thick, and the large leaves gather light efficiently. It is a premier choice for low light, and the variegated forms are particularly striking. It requires occasional pruning to keep it bushy.

2. **Pothos**
   Philodendron types

   Pothos and Cordatum have the smallest leaves of the Philodendron types. They are excellent in low light and require very little pruning. A 10 inch pot is sufficient for up to 6 years growth. Larger Philodendrons, while hardy, tend to be unmanageable.

3. **English Ivy**
   Hedera types

   Except for its susceptibility to pests, the English Ivy is strongly rooted, grows fast, and is easy to water. Cool locations suit it best. The larger leaved Marengo and Algerian Ivies are brightly variegated, while the smaller **helix** types often grow very exotic leaf shapes.

4. **Creeping Fig**
   Ficus pumila

   Like the Fig Tree, this cousin grows a dense mass of fine, fibrous roots. The root structure means fast growth and good tolerance to high light—but, if the roots ever dry out, the plant will disintegrate in 3-5 days. Eventually the stems thicken into a heavy trunk.

5. **Spider Plant**
   Chlorophytum comosum

   Because of its unusually thick and fleshy roots, the Spider Plant needs infrequent watering, and tolerates considerable neglect. The largest leaves often burn from low humidity, but the parent plant constantly produces new babies, which are more suited to dry conditions.

6. **Ferns**
   Nephrolepis, Asparagus

   Most Boston Ferns require a constant, multi-directional light source to retain all their fronds in good condition—but occasional trimming will keep up a good appearance. The Asparagus Ferns are less demanding, but will shed needles when too dry or too dark. The Ming Fern is by far the best.

7. **Hoya**
   Hoya species

   These heavy, waxy leaves tolerate all situations. The stems, too, are wiry and strong. When the plant flowers, it is easy to forgive the extreme slow growth. It requires only small amounts of water. To make it flower, keep it cool for 2 or 3 months in winter—then feed heavily.

8. **Prayer Plant**
   Maranta leuconeura

   Even though the leaf margins burn in low light or low humidity, the bright red and green markings make this plant the most exotic of the hangers. It grows fairly fast in average light and is easy to water. In 3 years the vines may reach 6' and support hundreds of leaves.

9. **Grape Ivy**
   Cissus species

   The Grape Ivy and Danish Ivy are somewhat delicate. In low light they become leggy, and they dislike abnormal temperatures. The Kangaroo Vine is hardier, but not nearly as tidy in appearance. After these vines mature, they are much easier to care for.

10. **Clerodendrum**
    Clerodendrum thomsonae

    This vine has exceptionally large leaves for the woodiness of the stem. The papery thin leaves are sometimes prone to pest attacks. Because it flowers so easily, it is worth the small amount of extra care. Heavy pruning is necessary in bright light to control size.

Hardy, Low Light Flowering Plants

Lighting accumulations for flowering plants.

Although flowering house plants normally need at least filtered window light to bloom (500 or more footcandles), some are spectacular in bright artificial light (100 fc). Even in a dark corner, a single spot light, burning 16 hours a day, is adequate for hardy plants. When only average artificial light is available (50 fc), the plants can be rotated to a window for 2-3 months a year—to initiate flower production.

Porous soil and constricted roots.

All tropical plants are easiest to keep, and grow fastest, in light, porous soil. Because flowering plants will drop their buds when the roots stay soggy for extended periods, good soil is a must. If the nursery soil is sandy, shake some from the rootball, and mix it with 50% perlite—then repot. Constricted roots are also a necessity for bountiful flowers. In a large pot, the plant grows roots first, foliage second, and flowers last. Only in bright light does a plant flower before it is rootbound.

Feeding schedules and seasonal lighting.

When a mature, healthy plant is reluctant to flower, it may need additional fertilizer. Always measure the directed dosage into 3 portions—spacing the applications over 4-6 weeks. If the plant still refuses to cooperate, a change in location nearly always works. Putting a well-lit plant in low light for 2-3 months, or a poorly-lit plant near a window for 1-2 months, often produces results. This method tricks the plant into thinking a seasonal change is occurring. When a window-flowering plant starts to show buds, wait until they are partially open before moving it to lower light—or they may drop off.

Extending the blossoming period.

Most of the pre-flowered pot plants (Chrysanthemum, Cyclamen, Gloxinia, Cineraria, Calceolaria) are meant to be thrown away when the blooms fade (2-6 weeks). The flowers last twice as long when the room temperatures are cool, and half again as long in high humidity. Notable for long indoor life are Azaleas, Miniature Roses, Aphelandras, Kalanchoes, Hibiscus, Citrus varieties, Gardenias and Geraniums. When these plants are given bright window light (500+ fc) for half the year, they can grow and flower for years.

THE 10 HARDIEST FLOWERING PLANTS

1. Peace Lily
   Spathiphyllum wallisii

   By far the best performer in low light, the **wallisii** flowers sporadically at 30 fc, while the larger **'Mauna Loa'** needs 50 fc. At 80 fc, a potbound plant will carry up to six flowers for at least half the year. Each flower lasts for three to four weeks.

2. Bromeliads
   Bromeliaceae

   Although Bromeliad flowers are best initiated at the nursery, the plants will maintain their blooms for four to six months—even in extreme low light (20 fc). **Aechmea fasciata 'Silver King'** has the largest, showiest flower. Discard the plant when the inflorescence is spent.

3. Bamboo Palm
   Chamaedorea erumpens

   Both Erumpens and the dwarf, Neanthe Bella, can be counted on to flower and fruit annually in 30 fc. The berries, borne low on the stalks, turn yellow, then purple. They last four to eight weeks. In bright light, a mature plant produces hundreds of the tiny fruits.

4. Lipstick Vine
   Aeschynanthus lobbianus

   All hanging basket-type plants with small oval leaves are noted for vigorous flower production. The best at 100 fc is the Lipstick Vine. The flowers are sturdy and long-lasting (three to four weeks), and the flowering period may last for two or three months, several times a year.

5. Christmas Cactus
   Schlumbergera bridgesii

   The mature specimens of Thanksgiving, Christmas, Easter and Orchid Cacti all bloom readily at 80 fc; however, they do prefer at least an East window. Individual flowers last two or three weeks, but, especially in lower light, the display goes on for several months.

6. Clerodendrum
   Clerodendrum thomsonae

   Even in 100 fc, these vines grow six feet a year. A plant in a 10 inch pot can cover an entire wall in three to five years. Delicate clusters of white, red-centered flowers contrast with the large, crinkly leaves. One variety has variegated foliage—in two-tone fluorescent green.

7. Flowering Maple
   Abutilon striatum

   These large, bell-shaped flowers last only a few days; but, in bright light, the plant is capable of producing them year around. At 100 fc there may be only a few at a time. The plain leaf variety is hardiest, but **thompsonii** is strikingly variegated and has orange flowers.

8. Crown of Thorns
   Euphorbia splendens

   In full sun, the flowers of this Succulent are bright red and vigorous. At 100 fc they are paler, almost pink. It often flowers after dropping most of its leaves. Left to ramble, its branches twist and twine into fantastic shapes. It will survive, but not flower, in 50 fc.

9. Asparagus Fern
   Asparagus 'Sprengeri'

   When rootbound, the **'Sprengeri'** may produce masses of tiny, fragrant white blooms—followed by long lasting, bright red berries. It prefers at least an East window, but 100 fc is easily sufficient for luxurious foliage. Regular feeding encourages flowering.

10. African Violet
    Saintpaulia varieties

    Any intensity of window light causes these small table plants to flower indefinitely. Even a leaf cutting will flower after three to five months. The more exotic-leafed varieties require more light, but the old favorites, **Ionantha** and **confusa**, can endure 80 fc.

Tall, Narrow, Upright Plants

Problems with a wide plant in a narrow space.

Shaping a Palm to fit against a wall.

Trimming back the excess foliage.

Shape control is easiest during the first few days.

The most restrictive growth habit of indoor plants is their width to height ratio. Modern building spaces frequently require a plant with a 5' to 8' height, but a spread of less than 3', preferably 2'. Only a few of the plants grow this way naturally.

When a wide plant is fit into a narrow space, without preliminary shape control, there is an unnatural loss in appearance. If the narrow space is a corner, the back leaves are bunched against the wall. Not only does the plant lose some of its character, but the rearward leaves start to burn after 2-4 weeks.

A widely spreading Palm is the most difficult shape to use in a small space. However, there is an excellent method for overcoming the difficulty. Most Palms are planted as a combination of different-sized plants in one pot. The designer need only be concerned with the largest plant. The largest plant will have 3-5 major fronds, with perhaps another spike starting to grow. The important observation is the direction of growth of the newest fronds.

At least 2 of them will fan out in a 60° arc. By cutting away all the smaller fronds on the side opposite the newest major fronds, the plant can be trimmed back up to 50% of the total growth—without materially affecting the appearance. Because the light source will be brightest away from the wall, most of the new growth will open up on the room side of the plant. And even if the plant looks a little skimpy initially, it will fill in within 2 or 3 months.

When any form of shape control is necessary to help a plant fit into a space, it should be done within a few days of installation—when the growth is still soft and fast. The soft growth readily takes to tying up or staking, and because the plant is fresh from the nursery, it will continue to grow fast for the first 2-4 months. After a plant has been indoors for awhile, its habits are much harder to change.

10 SUITABLE FORMS FOR TIGHT CORNERS

1. Bamboo Palm
   Chamaedorea erumpens

   The Bamboo's canes are so flexible, they can be squeezed together at soil level, so that a 7' plant is only 2' wide. Since this plant continuously produces new shoots at the base, it stays full from top to bottom. It tolerates the least light of all true uprights.

2. Yucca
   Yucca elephantipes

   Yuccas are usually grown as a series of different height canes per pot. The individual heads are less than 2' across, and the canes are easily moved in any direction. The cane-type **Dracaena massangeana** grows similarly, but the heads are slightly wider.

3. Indian Laurel
   Ficus retusa

   All Fig Trees can be grown as whips—rather than being severely pruned to develop a stout trunk. The Nitida (**retusa**) grows slower than the **benjamina**, so it is most often seen as a whip. They are attractive, and a 7' plant may be no more than 30 inches in diameter.

4. False Aralia
   Dizygotheca elegantissima

   This plant is nearly like the Bamboo Palm in overall appearance. The separate foliage groups have short stems, and the canes grow straight up and down. When the plant is over 8', the leaves get much larger, and the diameter spreads to 3 feet.

5. Spider Plant
   Chlorophytum comosum

   A well-grown, mature Spider Plant is 4 or 5 feet from top to bottom. Hanging in a corner, it can give the same effect as a False Aralia. It fills the space solidly; and the vines supporting the plantlets give it a long vertical line. The plain green variety grows longer runners.

6. Marginata
   Dracaena marginata

   Although this plant does not suggest a strong vertical appearance at the nursery, it does emphasize the long thin canes as soon as the leaves start to curve downward. The canes have a tendency to bend as the new growth forms. In time, the Marginata develops a new character.

7. Asparagus Fern
   Asparagus densiflorus 'Sprengeri'

   Similar to the Spider Plant, the Asparagus Fern grows strong vines that collapse over the edge of the pot—to support the weight of the foliage. These ferns may grow to 10' in length, and are an inexpensive way to achieve impressive size, in a narrow, linear form.

8. Corn Plants
   Dracaenas

   The **Dracaenas** are usually grown as 3 or more plants per pot, but if they can be obtained as singles, they form an exciting column of foliage that grows indefinitely, and will keep the leaves from tip to base in good window light. Warneckei is narrowest, followed by Janet Craig.

9. Split-Leaf Philodendron
   Monstera deliciosa

   The Split-Leaf needs to be staked to split satisfactorily, and in doing so, will become the narrowest of all vertical plant forms. With patience, the plant can be trained to any height. Other large-leafed Philodendrons also produce better foliage when staked.

10. Buddhist Pine
    Podocarpus macrophyllus

    The **Nagi** is narrower than the **macrophyllus**. Both of them, however, keep a narrow profile when produced as a single stem per pot. The branches of this plant can be pruned back, with only a small resultant loss in appearance. After reaching 8', they begin to bush out at the base.

Durable Groundcovers and Trailing Vines

The difficulty with planted-out groundcovers.

Methods for keeping them in their original pots.

Companion plantings.

The difference between trailers and fillers.

Groundcovers are the designer's best friend for creating a warm comfortable atmosphere with specimen plants. A single plant, standing on its own, may appear to be slightly artificial, but a groundcover can make it come to life, by helping to hide both the mulch and the plainness of the planter.

Groundcovers are also universally difficult to use. When planted together in the same pot with a large plant, there can be a problem with the groundcover drying out too quickly—especially in less than window light. At lower light levels, the large plant may dry half way down or more between waterings, and the groundcover suffers since it may only have roots in the upper 1/4 of the soil mass.

The best solution is to keep the small plants in their original containers. Then all the plants can be watered separately. This means extra maintenance in watering, but certainly less maintenance in trimming and replacements. There will always be a substantial net saving with this procedure. When the planter is too small to arrange the groundcovers around the pot containing the speciment plant, the 4 inch groundcover pots can often be 'dug into' the rootball without damaging the large plant.

It is possible to select groundcovers that can be planted and watered together with the major plant. If the major plant needs water approximately every 2 weeks, and dries half way down in the process, a Succulent groundcover will work perfectly. If the plant stays evenly moist, like a Fig Tree, a Creeping Fig or similar fast grower will work.

In large fixed planter gardens, the designer is often well advised to choose 2 groundcovers—one of them to hang over the planter's edge, and the other to fill in under the shrubs and trees. Both conditions are quite dissimilar, and often the light is much lower in the interior of the garden. Groundcovers are easy to control by pruning: their major limitation is durability.

10 STRONG, MULTI-PURPOSE VINES

1. Grape Ivy
   Cissus rhombifolia

   The most frequently used indoor groundcover, the Grape Ivy, even performs well in less than average artificial light (below 50 fc). It is excellent where root space is limited—such as a companion planting in a movable planter. A 4 inch pot will grow a huge plant with 6' runners.

2. English Ivy
   Hedera helix

   The English Ivy's advantage over the Grape Ivy lies in its ability to overhang a planter face—without the roots pulling out of the soil, under the weight of foliage. Its more aggressive roots make it suitable for planting out, together with Palms and thick leaved Trees.

3. Pothos
   Epipremnum aureum

   Like the Grape Ivy, the Pothos, too, has a problem with the foliage putting excess strain on the roots. But it also has the same advantage: a 4 inch pot will grow a huge plant. When used in a planter bed, each leaf grows its own roots, so the foliage gets much larger and sturdier.

4. Creeping Fig
   Ficus pumila

   This is the best plant for growing up a wall or cascading over the edge of a planter. It has the same vigorous roots as the Fig Tree. The stems have suction pads that adhere to any surface. Like the English Ivy, the vines eventually form a strong woody trunk.

5. Prayer Plant
   Maranta leuconeura

   The Prayer Plant is the perfect companion planting to specimen plants in big planters, in large brightly-lit open areas. They cover the planter bed up to a foot deep, and spill randomly over the edges. This plant can produce huge numbers of leaves per cubic foot.

6. Wandering Jew
   Tradescantia species

   Although this Vine is troublesome in a hanging basket, it roots from each leaf node that touches the ground in a planter. It is similar to the English Ivy, in that it can be planted out directly with Palms, and other plants with the same water requirements. It tends to take over in planter gardens.

7. Hoya
   Hoya species

   The Hoya is suitable as a groundcover with smaller plants. Its open pattern of growth matches angular shapes and delicate forms. It is tricky to water in artificial light, so is best left in the nursery container. The miniature **Hoya bella** is plain green but very finely textured.

8. German Ivy
   Senecio mikanioides

   In bright light and hot conditions, this Ivy is better than the English Ivies. It is easier to water and far less susceptible to pests. The glossy, semi-succulent leaves bring life to any planter. It tends to get leggy, so frequent pruning will encourage bushiness.

9. Succulents
   Succulent types

   Many small Succulents, that have no character on their own, will dress up the root surface of large Palms and Canes. Small Succulents aggressively propagate themselves, and prove to be hardy in all conditions. Good choices are ones with small leaves and thick, but trailing, stems.

10. Peanut Cactus
    Chamaecereus silvestri

    These long tubular Cacti lie flat on the soil surface—rooting all along their length and sending up new sprouts in profusion. From a distance, they look like a carpet of moss. They are effective companions to large Succulents like the Agave.

Dark, Rich-Green Leaves

Dark green leaves look healthy.

Dark, rich green leaves are perceived by the layperson to be the healthiest. The equation is understandable since outdoor plants appear greener against the blue sky or in contrast with the lighter exteriors of buildings. A dark green plant also has the least visible pattern of foliage. Its innocuous form supplies an acceptable choice for someone who is threatened by indoor plants.

They contrast to muted colors.

In an aggressive mode, dark green leaves are a vibrant contrast to most indoor furnishings. They are so dark that shadows won't reflect from their surfaces. This gives them a sharp-edged silhouette—sometimes too heavy in delicate surroundings—but where a focal point is needed amongst muted colors, the effect is immediately riveting.

They are enhanced by shiny surfaces.

To the designer, there is a richness in deep, dark green leaves that helps portray opulence. Whether the design theme feeling of expense is obtained through richly grained woods, or bright shiny brass, a dark green leaf lends its appeal equally. They are a natural.

Feeding deepens the foliage color.

Healthy tropical plants have richer colors when fed properly. This is not to suggest that indoor plants need a lot of food—they do not. But some plants, notably Palms, require extra iron or they develop chlorosis. A sure way to 'green up' all plants is by using organic food—either seaweed (preferably) or fish fertilizer. These plant foods contain many nutrients unavailable in chemically prepared fertilizers. Additionally, the organics can't burn the leaves.

Organic plant food is safe and effective.

Many modern composts are sterile, and while they provide the best aeration, they also run out of nutrients the fastest. Liquid seaweed can be used with every watering to assure a steady, if dilute, supply of food that promotes even growth. A standard fertilizer (like 20-20-20) can then be added 1-4 times a year depending on the light. Plants respond best when they are fed on a regular basis. The 20-20-20 can even be diluted for use every time along with the seaweed. Plants are like people—they prefer regular meals.

10 FLOOR PLANTS WITH DEEP GREEN LEAVES

1. **Janet Craig**
   Dracaena deremensis
   'Janet Craig'

   The Janet Craig stands ahead of all plants in its ability to maintain a dark, rich-green color in any light. Especially when planted 3-5 per pot, the leaves form a solid mass of green from top to bottom. The color is enhanced by frequent dusting.

2. **Schefflera**
   Brassaia actinophylla

   Like the Janet Craig, this plant is one large ball of leaves. Plants fresh from the nursery may be pale, but they soon 'green up' in interior lighting. If the leaves ever start to get mottled, suspect mites and spray immediately—and at least the new growth will be saved.

3. **Hawaiian Schefflera**
   Schefflera arboricola

   This dwarf Schefflera has thicker leaves than the Schefflera and they are a darker green. However, the dwarf plant is so much smaller, the overall effect is not as striking. In bright window light, this plant keeps its dark color better than most other tropical plants.

4. **Kentia Palms**
   Howea forsterana
   and belmoreana

   Since the Kentia is often chosen to live in average artificial light (50 footcandles), its foliage is thick enough to reflect all the light. Many plants look lighter green in bright light because the leaves are semi-transparent. Like most Palms, they need iron to keep their rich color.

5. **Peace Lily**
   Spathiphyllum species

   Whether the dwarf **wallisii** or the giant **'Mauna Loa'** is chosen, the Peace Lilies can be counted on to retain a rich, shiny green coat. The leaves are so smooth, they need only a monthly dusting and twice yearly cleaning to stay vibrant and alive. The **wallisii** is the greenest of the entire family.

6. **Indian Laurel**
   Ficus retusa

   A **Ficus benjamina's** leaves get thinner and paler as the light levels drop. The **retusa**, which looks identical, has leaves twice as thick, so they stay a dark green even in average artificial light (60 footcandles). This plant makes an excellent companion plant with the Hawaiian Schefflera.

7. **Holly Fern**
   Cyrtomium falcatum

   A well-grown, bushy Holly Fern carries the same strong green color as the outdoor Holly Tree. Boston Ferns alternately get lighter and darker between waterings, but the Holly Fern always stays the same color. Like all Ferns, it benefits from organic plant food like liquid seaweed.

8. **Burgundy Rubber**
   Ficus elastica 'Rubra'

   This dark ruby colored leaf is quite different from the more frequently used **'Decora'**. The dark color will fade by 50% in artificial light, but it is always darker than the other Rubber Tree varieties. Like other smooth skinned plants, frequent dusting and occasional cleaning enhances the color.

9. **Corn Plants**
   Dracaena fragrans and
   fragrans massangeana

   In the past, the **fragrans** was more widely used, but now the colorful **massangeana** is the most popular. The **fragrans** has a wide, long leaf that looks almost as rich as its cousin the Janet Craig—under low artificial lighting. The **fragrans** tolerates 25% less light.

10. **Coffee Tree**
    Coffea arabica

    Although this plant is not readily available in large sizes, 3' plants are quite attractive—with their luxurious, large drooping leaves. The plant tolerates bright artificial light, but grows much better in a humid window planter garden. Heavy pruning is required to keep it bushy.

Large, Exotic and Dramatic Leaf Forms

Indoor leaves grow larger because of reduced light.

Indoor plants having large leaves in the nursery will usually grow even larger leaves indoors. They do this as the granna rearranges itself to take advantage of the lower light. Because of this function, large leaves take on a character not seen outdoors. An 8' plant indoors may grow a leaf that would only be seen on a plant 5 times as large—in its native habitat.

They also become thinner.

Besides growing larger, the leaf also gets thinner, and in many cases becomes transparent enough to let the light shine through. The best example of this phenomenon is the Fiddle Leaf Fig. The Philodendron Selloum also takes on a delicate veined appearance indoors—even in good window light (300 fc).

Changes to the stems.

Enhancing the exotic appeal of large leaves, is the growth pattern of the stems supporting the foliage. They get thinner and longer. The result is a much weakened stem, attempting to support a giant leaf. The stem manages to do its job, but curves downward under the weight. Thus a plant which looks compact and sturdy at the nursery, will grow with grace after its first 6 months indoors.

Plants gradually alter their whole form.

Most tropical plants look much friendlier indoors than their strong stems would allow in the high light of the nursery. It takes about 2 years to completely regrow a tropical plant. During this time, the designer has ample opportunity to chart the direction of growth, and judiciously help the plant achieve its ultimate new form.

Selective pruning and long term growth.

When at all feasible, a plant should stay in the same location as long as possible—not because plants dislike being moved, but because plants develop a symmetry that corresponds to the direction of the light source. Left to its own devices, a plant will arrange its foliage attractively, spacing all the leaves so each gets its share of the light. Selective pruning makes sure they will be exactly where the designer wants them to be.

10 LARGE, ELABORATE LEAF STRUCTURES

1. Fiddle Leaf Fig
   Ficus lyrata

   When this plant reaches 10' tall, the newest leaves are at least 3'-4' long. In addition, they are deeply veined, corrugated, and distinctively fiddle shaped. At less than 100 fc, they become partially transparent. The long thin branches may arch downward 6' under the weight of the enormous leaves.

2. Striped Corn Plant
   Dracaena fragrans massangeana

   At 6' tall, the Bush Massangeana grows a wide, strap-like leaf, almost as long as the plant is tall. From a distance, this plant looks more massive than any other tropical of equal height. The lime green stripes fade only slightly in low light. A single large plant will completely fill an empty corner.

3. Schefflera
   Brassaia actinophylla

   Small floor plants are bushy, glossy and fat; and a 6' Shef supports new foliage clusters that are 2 feet in diameter. This plant looks best in bright artificial light, since sky and window lighting make the leaves face up or out—showing only the dull undersides. The plant diameter equals the height.

4. Selloum
   Philodendron selloum

   A thick trunk sprouts closely set, sturdy stalks, which terminate in ruffly, lettuce-like leaves. Some varieties are deeply palmated. In 100 fc, a 6' plant carries 20-50 leaves. These plants are extremely effective in high flying planters, where the light source is below the root mass.

5. Dumb Cane
   Dieffenbachia species

   As the plant grows taller, the leaves get larger—up to 3' long. Some varieties have more variegation than green in the foliage; other varieties are brightly mottled. The plant always directs its leaves downward, creating maximum visual display.

6. Rubber Tree
   Ficus elastica

   The most beautiful Rubber plants are standard forms—at least 8' tall. They carry hundreds of thick, uniform leaves. The stems and branches are heavy and straight. In bright sunlight, the crowns are dense. In 100 fc, the growth is more sculptural, and the leaves are thinner but larger.

7. Century Plant
   Agave

   Huge Agaves have stiff, strong leaves. The leaves of some varieties are cross-sectionally triangular. These plants exude power. They look indestructible. They are perfect as shrubberies in a Cacti planter. Many forms are highly colored—with silver, yellow, white, black and red.

8. False Aralia
   Dizygotheca elegantissima

   Smaller plants are distinctive enough, with bronze-black, tooth-edged leaves. But on reaching 10', the long narrow leaflets suddenly become 5 times as large as before. Since the large leaves grow at the top, this plant looks best from above.

9. Split-Leaf Philodendron
   Monstera deliciosa

   The juvenile form, **Philodendron pertusum**, shows only a hint of the mature plant's fantastic leaf designs. Holes appear at random in the leaves and the edges are deeply cut. This plant must be staked to produce dramatic leaf structures. It grows best in bark chips.

10. Staghorn Fern
    Platycerium species

    There are hundreds of different variations available on the Staghorn's unique antler-shaped fronds. The plant looks best hanging on a wall, but large plants are heavy and need considerable support. In maturity, the fronds may reach six feet in length.

Exciting, Multi-Colored Leaves

The availability of various color combinations.

Regrettably, the hardiest tropicals tend to be plain green. Some, however, produce all the colors of the rainbow, and a few, planted here and there, do much to lighten up an interior planting. Most colorful plants are small, and may have to be used as companion plantings to be effective. Brightly colored plants also need more light or the colors fade. All of them prefer sunlight to artificial light.

The most common ornamentation is variations of green and cream. The next in line is red, followed by light green, yellow and mauve. Since green and cream lead all other combinations by a wide margin, growers have been cultivating these varieties intensely, so that now many plants are nearly pure white.

Green and cream are the most common.

Fortunately, these plants need only 50% more light than an all green plant of the same genus. They always look dressed up. There are two separate variations of green and cream. Some plants have irregular blotches while others feature linear stripes. The designer will find it possible to do an entire design in variegated leaf forms, but it is best not to mix stripes with blotches.

Tricolored plants.

There is also quite a variety of green, cream and red combinations—called tricolors. Marginata, Maranta, Jade, Croton and Hoya are some of the easiest to find, but there are dozens of minor small plants that boast this exciting array of color. They are effectively used together in a small table arrangement, or in a low growing planter garden.

Using glazed planters with variegated foliage.

The best way to color up a plant arrangement, is by using a variegated plant with a plain groundcover in a hand thrown, glazed ceramic planter. All potters have their specialties in glazes, and the designer will find the artists exceedingly eager to make the exact color combinations the designer needs. The turn around time for custom pottery is surprisingly low (1-3 weeks), and they often cost little more than commercially produced ceramic planters—and certainly less than brass. Potters are an untapped resource to the designer.

10 BRIGHTLY-COLORED TROPICAL PLANTS

1. Croton
   Codiaeum

   Blushing reds, bright yellows, and many hues of green characterize the Croton. It puts on its most vivid color show in bright window light, but even in a North window, when the reds start to fade, it is still striking. **'William Craig'** is one of the most spectacular.

2. Copper Plant
   Acalypha wilkesiana macafeana

   The metallic crimson and bronze shadings make this a good shrub for high light planter gardens. When it gets bright window light, it grows fast and is easily pruned to any shape. In bright artificial light (100 fc), the colors pale out, but still retain their sheen.

3. Prayer Plant
   Maranta leuconeura

   With its dusky maroon undersides and its red-veined, variegated upper surfaces, the Prayer Plant looks just as elaborate from a distance as it does close up. Similar in shadings the **Calathea** (Peacock Plant). A faded variety **'Kerchoveana'** grows minus the red veins.

4. Rex Begonia
   Begonia rex

   Rex Begonias are the sturdiest of the large leafed Begonias. Others in the family are just as colorful. Like the Copper Plant, they brighten up a high light planter. The leaves grow half size in 100 fc, but the plants still retain their cheerful colors.

5. Bromeliads
   Bromeliaceae

   This large family has hundreds of different foliage color patterns. Many of them blush while flowering. Even the flowers have spectacular colors. **Cryptanthus** (Earth Stars) are a strongly colored, low growing plant, very similar in formation.

6. Flowering Maple
   Abutilon striatum

   The **thompsonii** variety, with fluorescent yellow and bright green leaves, is the most colorful of all the Flowering Maples. But even the ones with plain leaves have exotic flowers. Most of these plants will bloom year around in a planter garden with bright window light.

7. Hoya
   Hoya species

   Most Hoyas feature green and cream leaves, but **carnosa** varieties often have pink and rosy red shadings. Their smooth waxy surfaces make the colors look as if they are layered on. Hoya flowers are even more exotic than the foliage. They grow in white or pink clusters.

8. Tricolor Marginata
   Dracaena marginata 'Tricolor'

   While the regular Marginata's red-edged leaves are not very noticeable, the addition of the cream colored bands make the Tricolor the brightest low light plant of all. It retains its colors and grows strongly even in average artificial light (50 footcandles).

9. Flame Nettle
   Coleus varieties

   This diverse family makes good groundcover planting for high light gardens. The leaves are soft and thin, so high humidity is necessary for them to hold the leaves erect. In a very short time they will cover the entire planter bed with foliage.

10. Chocolate soldier
    Episcea cupreata

    Very few tropicals feature brownish leaves. This plant can be used as a high light groundcover, or in a hanging basket. It is not a 'hardy' vine, but frequent pruning will keep it in good shape for years. Cuttings root quickly in water. The flowers are a reddish orange.

Delicate, Feathery Foliage Patterns

Delicate foliage often needs humidity.

The group of plants with the most delicate leaves is also one of the hardest to care for. Delicate leaves usually mean a need for high humidity, and the designer will do well to give delicate leaves lots of light to make up for the lower indoor humidity levels.

Finely textured leaves suit window lighting.

Fortunately, delicate leaves look good in front of a window, where the light has many irregular spaces to shine through. The light penetration through the foliage mass also benefits the leaves away from the window. In many plants, a heavy concentration of leaves on the window side shades so much light, that those opposite grow weak and leggy.

Finely textured plants nearly all have the palest color foliage. A fine texture and a thin leaf are a common occurance with tropicals. The exception is all plants with needles. Plants with needles can be counted on to produce dusky, dark green colors.

Some plants look more delicate from a distance.

Two delicately textured plants deserve special mention—the Buddhist Pine and the Marginata. The Pine looks somewhat solid and overwhelming close up. It works best when approached from a distance. Its beauty lies in the gentle sway of the branches. The Marginata also looks like a mass of foliage close up, but at a distance, the regular curves of the leaves are emphasized by the often angular lines of the canes. The overall effect is one of easy motion and striking grace.

Architectural possibilities with small leaves.

All plants with masses of delicate leaves give the designer the opportunity for selective pruning—to achieve a more exciting architectural form. Branches can be cut away at random, only to increase the exotic appeal. Many of these plants are fast growers in good light, and should be reshaped annually. Canes that are too large should be cut off at the base. The other growth will quickly fill in the empty spaces. Protruding branches are best removed entirely, because plants frequently rely on the foliage tips for character.

10 EXAMPLES OF LIGHT, AIRY FOLIAGE

1. Ming Tree
   Polyscias fruticosa

   There is quite a variety of delicate Aralias produced in table sizes; the Ming is the only large specimen. A 10' plant is much coarser at the nursery than it eventually becomes indoors. This group of plants is renouned for ruffly-edged leaves, often exotically shaped.

2. Feathery Bostons
   Nephrolepis varieties

   'Whitmanii' and **'Rooseveltii'** Bostons grow so many thousands of crinkled leaflets, they look like eiderdown from a distance. Regular Bostons are sweeping and graceful, while the numerous feathery forms are impressive for their texture. All these feathery ferns are surprisingly hardy.

3. Pygmy Date Palm
   Phoenix roebelenii

   The Pygmy Date Palm stands out from other grass-like plants, because it grows in an orderly symmetrical fashion. From a distance it looks much like a large Boston Fern—light and airy. The Date Palm keeps its delicate looks even in bright window light.

4. False Aralia
   Dizygotheca elegantissima

   The False Aralia and the Ming Tree are a good match for overall appearance—they both have short stems and multitudes of small leaflets. Color-wise, they are at opposite ends of the green spectrum. The False Aralia is so dark it looks bronze to black in artificial light.

5. Marginata
   Dracaena marginata

   After it loses its stiff nursery leaves, the Marginata takes on the lilting appearance of the Date Palm. The leaves all arch away from the stem in a symmetrical ball. The Marginata looks best with at least three (preferably seven or more) plants per pot.

6. Buddhist Pine
   Podocarpus macrophyllus

   The **macrophyllus** species is as delicate as the **Nagi** is coarse. After the plant leaves the nursery, the branches start to droop and sway. Even though this plant is densely laden with needles in good light, the slender stems keep it looking soft and delicate.

7. Asparagus Ferns
   Asparagus varieties

   All of the Asparagus Ferns are delicate in their own way. The **'Sprengeri'** is the most bouffant, and full-blown plants appear as a hazy curtain from a distance. The **retrofractus** is more aggressive, even though its individual needles are very tiny and soft.

8. Maidenhair Fern
   Adiantum

   The Maidenhair is touchy outside a terrarium when small, but when the stems and leaves toughen (in an 8 to 10 inch pot), a single plant can cover a 2' diameter—in a sea of cascading miniature fronds. In bright light, the fronds are nearly transparent.

9. Silk Oak
   Grevillea robusta

   This is another touchy specimen. Like the Maidenhair, it keeps better when it gets larger (over 5'). It has a feel somewhere between a Buddhist Pine and a feathery Boston Fern. It combines the flexibility of the Pine's branches with the intense texture of the **'Whitmanii's'** fronds.

10. Mother Fern
    Asplenium bulbiferum

    From close up, this fern looks somewhat coarse, but from 6' away, the tiny plantlets growing all over the fronds give it an overall furry look. The Mother Fern is very hardy in artificial light (60 footcandles), and should be used more often.

Plants with Attractive Stems and Trunks

In some situations, the best part of a plant is its massive stem. Certainly the Fig Tree is renouned for its sturdy trunk. Large Palms often have shiny smooth trunks, and many of the Cane type plants have thick stems—highly ridged and attractively light brown.

Plants with larger stems need more light.

It is unfortunate that 2 plants of the same type, but with different stem thicknesses, are not equal in hardiness. The plant with the largest stem always needs more light. The more a plant is pruned at the nursery (or the faster it is grown), causes it to develop a thicker stem. Both of these growing situations are less conducive to an easy adjustment to life indoors.

Removing some foliage liberates the stem.

Many plants have beautiful stems hidden under masses of foliage. When the leaves are stripped back, a whole new character emerges. **Dracaenas** are a good example. Their stems turn light brown as they age and as the leaves are removed. Stems can add another dimension to a plant's form, and help to emphasize motion.

Loose bark indicates poor health.

Stems are also just as effective as the leaves in indicating overall health. The stem of a failing plant will start to shrink. The bark will get excessively wrinkled, even loose. It loses its naturally vibrant color, and frequently gets darker. A Fig Tree that is doing poorly will develop dark brown upper branches. This is a sure sign that the foliage on the branch will soon die.

Shrinking stems foretell eventual failure.

Plants that grow canes are usually the slowest to fail indoors. Sometimes the plant will carry a respectable head of leaves, even when the stem at the base is soft. A soft lower stem means the roots are already dead, and the only remaining life is in the upper stem. The plant should be discarded, or the growing tip propagated. Stems also indicate if a plant is getting enough light. If the stem narrows to 1/2 of its nursery size after coming indoors, the designer can tell the plant will fail within 6-12 months. Sometimes a stem is more descriptive than the leaves, when judging a plant's overall chances for long term survival.

10 LARGE TROPICALS WITH OUTSTANDING STEMS

1. Pygmy Date Palm
   Phoenix roebelenii

   This dwarf Palm grows a huge trunk in proportion to its height. In addition, the trunk is covered in thick, woolly brown fur. When the old fronds are trimmed off evenly, the combination of coarse brown wool with pale oval stubs, gives this plant an extra focus.

2. Marginata
   Dracaena marginata

   The Marginata will gently curve its slender stems naturally. Or, they can be elaborately trained at the nursery to produce a 'Marginata with Character'. These are usually 6' to 8' plants in a 14 inch tub, with 7 or more separate heads. The stems break out and up at right angles.

3. Bottle Palm
   Beaucarnea recurvata

   The grey, wrinkled, swollen basal growth on the Bottle Palm (or Pony Tail) curves upward gradually to a straight, sturdy stem. Mature plants may be 3' across at the base. When pruned, the plant develops multiple heads, that grow to produce an exotic series of new canes.

4. Crown of Thorns
   Euphorbia splendens

   Left to its own devices, the Crown of Thorns turns into a bramble patch of twisting, thorny stems. It can be trained into a Tree-shape by careful pruning. The stems are flexible enough to be conduced to grow in any direction. Topiary is one possibility.

5. Selloum
   Philodendron selloum

   Like the Pygmy Date Palm, the Selloum has an unnaturally thick stem for the size of the plant. When the lower leaves die back, the pruned stubs eventually fall away to uncover light colored 'eyes', set into the mahogany stem. Aerial roots add even more appeal.

6. Queen Palm
   Arecastrum romanzoffianum

   The Queen Palm is typical of smooth trunked palms. The trunks are thick and strong and taper gradually. Large specimen plants carry the leaves so high in the air, that only the trunk is visible at eye level. A 20' plant has a 6 to 8 inch trunk diameter.

7. Jade Plant
   Crassula argentea

   Even small Jades have an attractive, light skinned trunk. Large specimen plants are unique for producing the largest trunk—in relation to leaf size—of all tropicals. Indoors, Jades require regular pruning to stiffen the stems enough to carry their heavy weight of foliage.

8. Indian Laurel
   Ficus retusa

   Large Fig Trees are prized for their manly trunks, and although the Indian Laurel's is slightly thinner, it is decorated with light brown spots. Mature plants send down dark brown aerial roots that contrast smartly with the light grey skinned trunk.

9. Corn Plants
   Dracaenas

   As they age, and the lower leaves are lost, Corn Plants slowly develop a longitudinally fissured stem, decorated with horizontal leaf scars. Massangeana is the most beautiful. The cane types of these plants may have 2 inch diameter circular stems, similar to the Yucca.

10. Rubber Plant
    Ficus elastica

    Although from close up, the Rubber Plant's trunk and branches are not as attractively decorated as some of the other **Ficus**, its open pattern of branches and relatively few leaves give it the most visible support structure of all large tropical plants.

Traffic-Hardy Tropical Plants

Traffic-hardy plants need flexible leaves.

The number one requirement for traffic-hardy plants is a firm attachment between the leaf and the stem. The second need is to resist shedding and burning at the leaf tips. The worst plants for well-traveled areas are those like the Warneckei—whose leaves fall away at a touch, and brittle plants like the Schefflera—whose leaves crack and snap off when abused.

The tough, durable tropicals can be jostled a hundred times a day, and feel better for the experience—than the humans involved. Most people do not like to run into indoor plants for two reasons. They are both annoyed the plant is in the way, and they sometimes fear the plant will be damaged.

Even though the designer tries to keep plants away from traffic areas, and there are times during the day when a space is heavily populated, it may only happen for 5% of the day's total hours. When unoccupied, the space may look exceedingly bare.

Using plants in heavy traffic areas.

Accordingly, the plants listed on the opposite page are as durable as they look. Many are also outdoor-looking plants. People seem to be less threatened when a durable appearance is combined with a temperate zone formation, than by some of the more exotic tropicals. There are always people who feel that plants are out of place in a commercial environment, but by keeping away from the tropical look, the designer can easily overcome these objections.

Temperate zone look-alikes are often the best choices.

When less durable plants must be used in places where they are certain to suffer mechanical damage, an allowance should be made for additional maintenance costs. Palms, with their spreading habit, and often grass-like foliage, are susceptible to tip burn. Not only will the Palms require 2 or 3 times as much maintenance, but they may need replacing on an annual basis. Gradually, as the foliage is trimmed back, they begin to look unhealthy and unattractive. It is interesting to note that most people respect a healthy-looking plant, but feel free to abuse an already beat-up specimen.

Mechanical damage and maintenance costs.

THE 10 TOUGHEST PLANTS FOR HEAVY TRAFFIC

1. Fig Tree
   Ficus benjamina

   Durable leaves, flexible branches, and fast growth make this Tree the universal choice for well-traveled areas. Most of the other **Ficus** are also durable, although the **'Decora'** leaves sometimes crack. Long, flexible branches are superior to stout, thick limbs.

2. Yucca
   Yucca elephantipes

   Some Yucca varieties have stiff, serrated leaves that can scratch bare flesh. **Aliofolia**, especially when grown in less than 300 fc, develops a softer, downward curving leaf. The foliage is nearly impossible to tear off, but cane types need to be well-rooted, or staked to prevent tipping over.

3. Fan Palms
   Chamaerops, Livistona

   All Fan Palms are extremely tough. Their small stiff fronds, short stems, and thick trunks give them a sturdy silhouette. Sometimes, repeated brushings will burn the tips of the fronds. This is easily corrected by trimming. Sago Palms (**Cycas**) are also good choices.

4. Buddhist Pine
   Podocarpus macrophyllus

   This graceful plant features long, flexible stems and small, flattened needles. Occasionally, the stems get too soft and must be pruned part way back. If not, the branches will bend down to the floor under their own weight. Some species have softer needles, but all are excellent plants.

5. Hawaiian Holly
   Leea coccinea

   Even though the leaves are very soft—almost succulent—they are securely attached. There is a possibility of tip burning in high traffic areas, but growth is rapid and new shoots grow continually from the base and stems—especially in good light over 300 fc.

6. Lady Palms
   Rhapis excelsa & humilis

   Both **excelsa** and **humilis** are difficult to damage. Tip burning is more common with them than with Fan Palms. Also, trimming the hundreds of fronds on a large plant can be time consuming. However, this Palm suckers freely, and the stems are slim but durable.

7. Stiff Leafed Lilies
   Aspidistra, Clivia
   Sansevieria

   Hardy Lilies attach their stiff leaves directly to large underground roots. Well-rooted plants can take abnormal abuse without showing any damage. Sansevieria has the most durable leaves, Clivia is the most securely rooted, and Aspidistra has the most flexible foliage.

8. Peace Lily
   Spathiphyllum wallisii

   Although this Lily has soft, flexible leaves, the plant is hardy because it produces new foliage quickly, and it features a massive root mass for the size of the plant. The leaf tips do burn, but they are easily trimmed. **'Clevelandii'** and **'Mauna Loa'** are larger and more delicate.

9. Woody Vines
   Hedera, Ficus

   The best Vines for heavy traffic have woody stems and stiff leaves. English Ivy has the strongest leaves, and the Creeping Ficus has the better roots. Poorly rooted Vines can pull out of the soil. After their stems have turned thick and brown, these plants have matured.

10. Leathery Ferns
    Rumohra, Cyrtomium

    Most Ferns bruise easily, but leather-leafed types perform much like miniature Palms. The Leather Fern is especially hard to damage. The fronds are almost plastic to the touch. The Holly Fern grows much larger, but the stems can snap when bent severely.

Chlorine Tolerant Plants for Pools

Chlorine gas burns the leaves of most tropicals.

The chlorine fumes from swimming pools can quickly destroy most tropical plants. The problem is ameliorated when the air is exchanged at least once an hour. Nevertheless, only a few tropicals can stand at a pool's edge and breathe the fumes 24 hours a day, 7 days a week. The key plants in this group feature tough, low moisture leaves. A partial exception are the Succulents, which may burn around the leaf edges, but otherwise survive quite well.

The survivors benefit from the high humidity.

The plants that can survive the fumes are greatly benefited by the increased humidity. They grow much better (given the same light intensity) than they would in a normal indoor space. The Warneckei is one of the best examples. The leaves get brighter and suckers grow readily at the base of the stems.

Pool area plants need frequent cleaning.

One danger to a plant near a pool is chlorinated water splashing on the leaves. Continued splashing eventually burns the leaf surfaces. All plants around pools and saunas need to be rinsed off at least once a month, even if they are not being splashed. When they are not rinsed frequently, the dust build up seems to attract the chemical—stunting the growth.

Bromeliads are in their natural environment.

The best plants of all, and ones that suit waterfalls or paneled walls—are Bromeliads. The high humidity nearly duplicates their natural environment, where they live high on trees and get most of their moisture from the air. The Bromeliads will rarely ever need water, and flowers seem to last forever. Furry leaved Bromeliads are not quite so good, especially if not washed off frequently.

The high humidity of a pool area gives the designer a flexibility in plant choices beyond the scope of normally hardy tropicals. As long as the plants have a hard, shiny leaf surface, with a low moisture content, they will be excellent choices. If a plant is not chlorine tolerant, it will show it, by burning within the first two weeks.

10 PLANTS WITH THE BEST QUALITIES FOR POOL AREAS

1. Warneckei
   Dracaena deremensis 'Warneckei'

   The Warneckei is an unlikely candidate for a pool area, but the leaves are just leathery enough to resist the chlorine. The humidity brightens the colorations, and the leaves stay erect and stiff—rather than drooping as they would in equivalent light in an office.

2. Sansevieria
   Sansevieria trifasciata

   Even when this plant is repeatedly splashed with highly chlorinated water, the leaves remain unmarked. It is especially valuable if there is heavy traffic around the pool, since it can be knocked over, out of its pot, without suffering physical damage or a check in growth.

3. Aspidistra
   Aspidistra eliator

   A little less durable than the Sansevieria, the Aspidistra may occasionally burn at the tips until the new growth forms. The new leaves adapt to the chlorine and burn less. Also, like the Sansevieria, it is extremely tolerant to physical abuse and handling.

4. Bromeliads
   Bromeliaceae

   These tough leaves are not bothered by the fumes in the least. The advantage here, is that this plant luxuriates in high humidity, and can be mounted anywhere, even without any roots, and still look good for a long time. It may never need watering.

5. Bottle Palm
   Beaucarnea recurvata

   Large Bottle Palms (over 3') have heavier leaves than smaller specimens, and survive best. Sometimes the high chlorine levels burn the new emerging growth on younger plants. This plant may only need water every three months if the humidity is high.

6. Agaves
   Agave types

   These large spreading plants are suited to a pool space where the focal plane is at floor level. They naturally look as if they should grow out of the floor. Some of the larger Agave species have sharp pointed leaves, that may pose a problem to children.

7. Yucca
   Yucca elephantipes

   The Yucca often develops mildew in high humidity, but the chlorine seems to keep it in check. Chlorine also prevents pest attacks on tropical plants, and there is rarely ever a problem around a pool. Scale is the most resistant to chlorine, mites are the least.

8. Hawaiian Holly
   Leea coccinea

   With its soft succulent foliage, the **Leea** needs to be at least 5' from the pool edge to do well. Even so, there may be some yellowing of the leaf edges. Still, the humidity produces fast bushy growth, and the plant is far superior to the Fig Tree in performance.

9. Rubber Tree
   Ficus elastica 'Decora'

   The Rubber Tree should do better than it does, but the chlorine checks the growth and yellows the leaf margins, unless the tree is 10' back from the water's edge. Then it does well—even if the light is quite low (50 footcandles or more).

10. Clivia
    Clivia miniata

    This Lily makes a good small shrub. The deep green leaves contrast well with the sparkling water. The plant stays short, so it can be used beneath taller plants in a corner garden. The leaves resist all but the most vigorous handling and accidental damage.

Plants for Hot, Bright, Dry Conditions

Tropical plants grow naturally in 2 broad ranges of climate. Some favor humidity, while others prefer heat. Hot, sunny and dry weather suits most Palms and Canes. Indoors, however, these conditions are universally difficult—even for the Palms and Canes.

Plants growing outdoors rarely have year around heat.

Outside, most tropicals are blessed with either a cooler rainy season, or high average yearly humidity. Plants in highly humid geographic areas rarely have the intense heat of savannah-like places. And even those tropical plants that are forced to suffer through summer heat, are always given the chance to recover when the season changes.

Only indoors is there no relief from low humidity. The unrelenting dryness causes a huge demand for water at the roots—to offset transpiration. Then, when winter comes, and the light intensity reduces by one-half, the plant is torn between the continued need for moisture, and a slowdown in growth. The net result is a form of wilting—only common to indoor plants in bright light and low humidity.

Low humidity causes the foliage to wilt.

High temperatures and low humidity also bring with them the problem of pests. Spider mites, particularly, do not breed in temperatures below 65°F. But in 80° to 90°F dry heat, their populations will increase more than 1 million times—in 30 days.

Pests breed quickly in hot, dry atmospheres.

The mites also breed in high humidity, but the plant suffers less because it is growing more vigorously. Pests can make short work of a plant when the conditions are right. If possible, plants growing in a hot window should be sprayed once or twice during the summer (especially the thin-leaved types).

Sometimes maintenance personnel have a difficult time spotting the onset of a pest attack. There is one easy infallible method. A plant under attack will suddenly reduce its demand for water. This happens suddenly, within 2 or 3 weeks. Always suspect pests when a healthy looking plant starts acting strange. When it starts dropping leaves (after 4-8 weeks), it may be too late to recover the plant without extensive greenhouse hospitalization.

Spotting pest attacks by monitoring water usage.

10 CHOICES FOR HEAT, LIGHT AND LOW HUMIDITY

1. Cacti
   Cactus genera

   Small Cacti—more than large Peruvian or Barrel specimens—are less prone to scorch in full sun. The larger Cacti, however, withstand the heat and dryness better. Cacti in these conditions will all flower readily. The Peruvian Cactus is the most spectacular.

2. Succulents
   Succulent types

   Large, leather leafed Succulents scorch less often than the thinner skinned, thick leaf types. They also endure the heat and low humidity easier. Most Succulents are easy to flower in bright light. Often the smallest types have the largest, most colorful blooms.

3. Yucca
   Yucca elephantipes

   This plant thrives in the heat. It has a well developed root system that can easily supply as much moisture as the foliage needs. In bright light, growth is rapid for such a durable leaf structure. Spikes of creamy white flowers are common in over 1000 fc.

4. Bottle Palm
   Beaucarnea recurvata

   The Bottle Palm has a Cactus-like bulb at its base. It stores enough water to last the plant for at least 3 months—even in extremely drying conditions. Large plants over 6' grow multiple heads and long, spiraling, fantastically twisted, narrow, coarse leaves.

5. Fan Palms
   Chamaerops, Livistona

   Since Fan Palms have relatively high root/foliage ratios for Palms, they rarely dry out. Dry air sometimes promotes spider mites, but they are easy to spray. Palms with soft, grass-like fronds are poor candidates for dry atmospheres. The Areca and Roebelenii Palms are the worst.

6. Stiff Leafed Lilies
   Aspidistra, Sansevieria

   Because the leaf joins directly to the thick roots, these Lilies have little difficulty in storing and supplying water for the foliage. The Sansevieria is very tough, and prefers high heat and light. The colorations are bright, and the plant continually sprouts new suckers.

7. Fig Tree
   Ficus benjamina

   Even though Fig Trees tend to wilt in the heat, they gradually adapt their leaves to retain more moisture. Other varieties, like the Rubber Plant, also change their leaf structures. They will all survive if given enough water. Pests are sometimes a problem in dry heat.

8. Selloum
   Philodendron types

   Philodendrons with large leaves and thick stalks are surprisingly slow to wilt in hot, dry conditions. Full sun, however, often scorches the oldest growth. The Split-Leaf is good, but the Selloum is much better. Smaller leafed types tend to dry out faster than the roots can pump water.

9. Lipstick Vine
   Aeschynanthus types

   The Lipstick is typical of a few Vines that have semi-succulent leaves. These leaves can store enough water to counteract dry air. Heat does not bother them too much, and they can eventually adapt to all but the brightest of full summer sun. In bright sun, the foliage wilts—even with wet roots.

10. Reflexa
    Dracaena reflexa

    All **Dracaena** types suffer to a degree in bright sun, because the roots cannot supply enough water to offset evaporation. Pests are sometimes a problem, too. The Reflexa has the smallest leaves and consequently is the best choice. Warneckei is also good.

Plants that Tolerate Cold and Dampness

Cool temperatures check the new growth.

Cool, damp conditions are tolerated by tropical plants that have neither papery thin leaves or soft succulent foliage. A cool, damp environment slows down growth, and makes papery leaved plants like the Fig Tree shed, because the foliage cannot dry the roots out fast enough. Soft, succulent plants are also fast growers, and they can quickly start to rot in cool moist places.

Fleshy leaves suffer the most.

The best plants for these conditions have hard leaves—thick and strong without being fleshy. The two Ferns, Boston and Asparagus, are opposites. The Asparagus has hard needles compared to the Boston's delicate fronds, and consequently, it tolerates temperatures down to near freezing. Temperatures nearly down to freezing will burn fleshy foliage just as the sun does. Sunscorch dries out the leaf and burns it, while low temperatures freeze the internal moisture. The consequence of both situations is a similar-looking patch of destroyed tissues, one brown and the other black.

Some tough-leaved tropicals prefer low temperatures.

Sometimes the designer is faced with a lobby that can be counted on to be cool for most of the year. This makes plants like the Pittosporum suitable—a plant normally not hardy enough for average indoor conditions. Plants in this category have extremely tough fibrous leaves with little internal moisture. These plants fail quickly at normal temperatures because they cannot adapt their root systems and foliage enough to use water before the roots fail from overwatering.

Dampness encourages mildew on rough textured foliage.

Dampness disadvantages other plants that would normally seem to be good candidates—given their hard, low-moisture foliage. These plants, like the Yucca, have just enough surface leaf texture to encourage the growth of mildew. Plants in cool, damp conditions perform much better if the light is at least 300 footcandles, and if there is adequate movement of air.

10 CHOICES FOR COOL, HIGH HUMIDITY AREAS

1. Cacti
   Cactus genera

   Cacti stand up well to all extreme conditions, and cool temperatures are no exception. They will grow much slower than they do in hot, bright conditions, but still last indefinitely. Smooth, thin-skinned Cacti are more susceptible to freezing than barrel and globular shapes.

2. Asparagus Ferns
   Asparagus varieties

   All Ferns are good choices for cold, drafty areas. The family of Asparagus Ferns is best because they have hard needles, rather than papery thin fronds. The variety, **'Sprengeri'**, will not burn even when the thermometer dips to freezing. Other Ferns prefer at least 40°F.

3. Pittosporum
   Pittosporum tobira

   A number of plants can stand to live indoors, but have difficulty in temperatures over 65°-70°F. The Pittosporum is a good example. Others include the Azalea and similar plants with extremely woody stems. All plants in this class prefer good window lighting for strong growth.

4. English Ivy
   Hedera helix

   Ivies are like Ferns in their preference for cooler indoor temperatures. Higher temperatures encourage pest attacks and excessively dry the foliage. Even the Grape Ivies can stand considerable coolness, although their thin leaves fare less well when dampness accompanies the cold.

5. Norfolk Pine
   Araucaria heterophylla

   A Norfolk Pine will grow in less light when the temperature is lower. Like the Pines and Ferns with needles, their foliage is woody, and its low moisture content makes them less suitable to heat. These plants also stand drafts and dampness exceptionally well.

6. Fan Palm
   Livistona chinensis

   These indestructible Palms are nearly as good as Cacti in their ability to survive heat and cold. Because the leaf surface is smooth, they are not bothered by mildew. All Fan Palms easily endure temperatures as low as freezing. Extended periods of dampness will check the growth.

7. Screw Pine
   Pandanus species

   This **Dracaena** look-alike is much more durable. While cold burns a **Dracaena's** tissues, the Screw Pine has practically no internal foliage moisture. The Screw Pine is excellent in cool lobby entrances, but the foliage is serrated, and should be kept away from traffic areas.

8. Rubber Tree
   Ficus elastica 'Decora'

   For a plant with rather thick fleshy leaves, the Rubber can stand temperatures down to near freezing without even harming its new growth. It has a very thick, tough outer skin that protects the delicate tissues inside. Other **Ficus** varieties, like the **benjamina**, start to drop buds below 60°F.

9. Aspidistra
   Aspidistra eliator

   The Aspidistra's name appears in connection with nearly all difficult indoor conditions. It can survive down to 40°F, but does not have a thick enough skin to go as low as the Rubber Tree. Other Lily forms like the Clivia are also good in the cold. They also resist mildew caused by dampness.

10. Succulents
    Succulent types

    The best Succulents for the cold have the least fleshy leaves. However, a plant like the Jade can have some of its leaves damaged by freezing and grow new ones when the temperature is raised. A Succulent's roots survive cold better than the foliage does, and generate new growth quickly.

Slow Growing Table Centerpieces

*Dwarf plants
make good decorations.*

Often the designer needs a small plant, that stays the same size for long periods. The choices are either natural dwarfs, or slow growers. The plants on the opposite page are a combination of both, and they are especially good because they look full-grown at table size. The foliage is small and delicate and they give the effect of the bonsai.

*The Peace Lily
has many uses.*

The one exception is the Peace Lily. This is a rare specimen among tropicals. The leaves always grow to the same length (under one foot), and if the plant ever gets too bushy, it can be thinned out or divided. Its ability to flower in artificial light doesn't hurt its position as the most usable of all small plants. The Peace Lily is a fast grower, and can have hundreds of leaves in an 8 inch pot. But whether it has 20 leaves or 100 leaves, it looks much the same.

The plants in this group are equally at home on a reception desk or on a bookcase shelf. They are all quite sturdy, and except for the Bird's Nest, can be moved from place to place—without worry about adjusting to the new conditions. This is valuable when flower arrangements and seasonal color are occasionally used to replace the green foliage plants.

*Considerations for
a table-top plant.*

When the designer is choosing plants for a table centerpiece, there are two important considerations; the rootball should be small, and the foliage should extend over the edge of the planter. In addition, plants that form rosettes, or grow equally away from the center, will be pleasing in all situations.

*Some immature plants
have limited usefulness.*

There are many tropicals that make good table plants. Some are brightly colored, and often have long-lasting flowers. Many large tropicals, like the Marginata and Dieffenbachia, look good when small. They last up to a year on a table, and are easily transferred to a floor location after their usefulness has passed.

THE 10 HARDIEST FLOWERING PLANTS

1. Peace Lily
   Spathiphyllum wallisii

   The Peace Lily will get bushier without getting taller. In average artificial light (60 fc), it doubles in size every 2 or 3 years. It is easy to cut the rootball in half if the plant gets too large. The leaves stand considerable handling without marking. Remove old leaves when they start to burn.

2. Leather Fern
   Rumohra adiantiformis

   The toughest and slowest growing of all Ferns, the Leather Fern needs 3-5 years in low light (30 fc), to double in size. Its foliage can be cut and used in floral bouquets, where the fronds will outlast the flowers. The dark green fronds are attractive in any setting.

3. Bird's Nest Fern
   Asplenium nidus

   This pale green beauty uncurls new fronds slowly, each one just slightly larger than the one before. Although it is delicate and prefers not to be moved, it will perform well close to a window. It can stay in the same pot for at least 3 years, while doubling in size.

4. Bonsai
   Bon ai

   Some of the Bonzai Pines mass-produced today hold up well in warm indoor temperatures. They seem never to grow, and if they can be kept cool for part of the year, they last indefinitely. They have durable leaves and stems, and can be moved around in any reasonable light.

5. Bromeliads
   Bromeliaceae

   Some Bromeliads are primarily valuable for their flowers which last up to six months. Other Bromeliads (**Tillandsias**) are mounted on bits of weathered wood. They are fuzzy and delicate and need only an occasional misting. Colorful leaves are the attraction of still another group.

6. Bottle Palm
   Beaucarnea recurvata

   Although the plant gets large in time, it grows slowly. Even 1' plants have a thickened basal growth—topped by a delicate tuft of narrow curving leaves. It can survive months without water, and rivals the Leather Fern in ability to withstand extreme conditions.

7. Meyer Fern
   Asparagus densiflorus 'Meyers'

   This Asparagus Fern grows short, fat, furry fingers of needles. In time they get 2' long. The individual foliage groups head off in random directions, held up by a sturdy stem. This plant should have fairly bright light (over 80 footcandles) to perform well.

8. Desert Rose
   Aeonium types

   Quite a few **Aeoniums** grow to form a rosette of petals that look like fleshy green flowers. Pruning them produces branches, and a 1' tall plant can have a dozen 'flowers' at the same time. They are easy to grow but need window light to flourish.

9. Bird's Nest Sansevieria
   Sansevieria 'Hahnii'

   This plant is as durable as its taller brother the Snake Plant. New varieties on the market are brightly variegated, and are often planted 3-5 to a cluster. It fares well even in very low artificial light (25 footcandles). The plant stays short forever.

10. Cacti Gardens
    Cactus species

    Small bowls planted with a variety of miniature Cacti make an unusual centerpiece. Trailing Succulents can be added for groundcovers. The Old Man Cactus, with its coat of white fur, looks good as the specimen plant in the grouping.

Tropical Plants that Stay Short

The tropicals in this group are useful—as shrubs in planter gardens—as low area dividers—and to fill spaces where short and bushy is a premium. Four of the plants are Palms—slow growing Palms that may only increase their height by 6 inches a year, although in time they outgrow the space. Only the Hawaiian Shef needs height control to curb fast growth.

Planter garden shrubs should grow slowly.

Shrubberies are the most difficult selection the designer must make to create a planter garden. The groundcovers dutifully lay flat on the ground, while the tall specimen plants are usually encouraged to get larger. The shrubs, though, must look the same indefinitely—to avoid becoming messy and overgrown.

Long term growth habits are equally important.

Indoor planter gardens are too frequently designed to look good on installation—without concern for long term growth. It is only the judicious use of shrubs that can control an eventual tangled mass of foliage. In outdoor gardens, where the specimen plants reach great heights, the shrubs may get 10' tall and still look in scale. Indoors, a garden needs an organized uniform growth—on a human scale.

Creating an unbroken line of equal-sized plants.

In mass plantings, whether in fixed or moveable planters, uniform-height foliage, beneath eye level, draws the eye gently along the contour. Often the designer may specify an unbroken line of plants—from a half dozen to a hundred or more. To best maintain this effect, all plants must be absolutely identical to start. They should be hand selected for similarity in trunk caliber and ratio of roots to soil—to make sure they all grow at the same rate.

Rotational cycles for uniform growth.

When the light is variable throughout the length of the planting, the plants are easily kept the same size through a quarterly rotation. A longer cycle than 3 months will give the plants in the highest light a burst of growth that may never be duplicated by the lower light units.

10 USEFUL SHRUBS FOR FILLERS

1. Neanthe Bella
   Chamaedorea elegans

   The Neanthe Bella may reach 6' indoors, but only after at least 5 years. Normally, it levels off at 4'. Even in low artificial light (30 fc), it looks good, although it needs 60 fc to stay bushy. It is the best commercial dwarf Palm for all situations.

2. Chinese Evergreen
   Aglaonema species

   The Chinese Evergreen may also reach 6' or more eventually, but 4' is usually the maximum height. A 2' plant in a 10 inch planter takes 3-5 years to become 4' tall. It is content to produce new suckers at the base—rather than increase in height. It is low light hardy.

3. Pygmy Date Palm
   Phoenix roebelenii

   Because the Date Palm grows so slow, it is suitable where low growth is needed. It keeps on growing, and may get over 10' tall after 8-10 years. Besides its attractive head of fronds, it has a stout, oversized, hairy trunk that makes it appear to be stunted.

4. Hawaiian Schefflera
   Schefflera arboricola

   This plant grows its branches to enormous length, but they are so heavy the stems cannot support them. If they are left unstaked, they will grow horizontal to the ground. The small leaves give the appearance of a dwarf plant. Yearly pruning keeps it short for more than 5 years.

5. Aspidistra
   Aspidistra eliator

   An Aspidistra in a 10 inch pot will grow for more than 5 years before the roots outgrow their space. During that time, the plant will add 5 or 10 new leaves each year. In good light, the plant's overall height will be between 2½ and 3½ feet.

6. Jade Plant
   Crassula argentea

   A commonly available form of this plant is 2 or 3 feet tall in a 5 gallon pot. Indoor growth is lateral rather than vertical. After 5 years, it may get one foot taller, but more often, the branches become pendulous. Frequent pinching back encourages inner growth.

7. Clivia
   Clivia miniata

   As a houseplant, the Clivia is prized for its yearly show of flowers. As a commercial plant, it is important because of its durability and tolerance to low light. Plants taller than 2' are rarely available. As the plant ages, it produces dozens of suckers.

8. Snake Plant
   Sansevieria trifasciata

   Some commercially produced Sansevierias are over 4' tall. The dozens of stiff spikes make this a valuable specimen for any difficult indoor situation. Sansevieras grow much like the Aspidistra. The latter takes less light, but the former is more durable.

9. Fan Palms
   Livistona, Chamaerops

   Fan Palms grow slower than the Date Palm. They may only produce 2 or 3 new leaves every year. The foliage is sometimes too coarse for richly ornamental interiors, but they make great plants for forgotten corners and hideaways.

10. Sago Palm
    Cycas revoluta

    The Sago looks like a coarse Date Palm, but grows even slower than a Fan Palm. Unless it grows in bright window light, the designer can count on no more than 1 foot of growth every three years. The Sago has the stiffest foliage of all tropical plants.

Eye-Level Indoor Plants

Comparing the different sizes of plants.

The casual observer relates to plants in a variety of ways—depending on size. A table centerpiece looks like a simple decoration, a 3' plant is like a garden shrub—hardly noticeable, a 5' plant is just large enough so that the observer still feels bigger and in control, a 7' plant towers overhead and may be a strong focal point or a hulking menace, and a 10' plant is so large it has a character all its own.

The 3 most common North American floor plants.

Five foot plants are the commonest floor plants available at the retail level, and the size most identifiable by the passerby. They are conveniently planted in a 10 inch pot, and over 50% of all units sold in North America are Arecas, Schefflacker, and Fig Trees.

Problems with these 3 plants.

The designer will improve an indoor planting by staying away from these 3 overused varieties as much as possible—not only because they are visible everywhere, but also because they are extremely troublesome at this size. The Fig Tree is overpruned and hard to water, and both the Areca and Schefflera are still juveniles. Their soft foliage and underdeveloped roots mean they are fragile, hard to water, and susceptible to pests.

Fortunately, there is an excellent array of exotic, seldom seen specimens in the 5' range. They are often hardy and slow growing. They may cost 2-4 times as much as the Fig Tree, but will change any interior plant design from ordinary to exciting.

Using a tall, narrow planter for long term height control.

Plants of this size lend themselves to a tall, narrow decorative container (24 in. tall x 14 in. diameter) that has groundcover spilling over the edge. The tall container boosts the height without increasing the plant cost, and the groundcover softens its stark sides. The unit will also fit into a narrow space, and the planter itself helps to emphasize vertical motion. If the plant is a type that grows upward, and height control is a problem, the nursery container has at least 1 foot of space underneath that allows for gradually lowering the plant.

10 OUTSTANDING AVERAGE-SIZED PLANTS

1. **Peruvian Cactus**
   Cereus peruvianus

   This Cactus has a strong, smooth-ribbed exterior, that is not as threatening as most Cacti. It needs good window light to prevent the stems from narrowing to a point. This is an exciting plant for an unexpected corner. It flowers in bright window light.

2. **Mauna Loa**
   Spathiphyllum
   'Mauna Loa'

   The largest of the Peace Lilies, the **'Mauna Loa'** is striking with its giant dark green leaves and huge white flowers. It grows much like a tall Aspidistra. Although perfectly at home in average artificial light, it flowers more than half the year in over 150 fc.

3. **Massangeana Cane**
   Dracaena fragrans
   massangeana

   Four to six feet is the most popular size for this unusual plant. Its bright leaves hang easily from ramrod-straight canes. The Massangeana shows the most color of all narrow upright plants produced in a 10 inch planter. It is useful in any location from low to high light.

4. **Rubber Plant**
   Ficus elastica 'Decora'

   Standard form, 5' Rubber Plants, with their stout trunk and branching limbs, look like an overgrown bonsai. But, with their oversize leaves, they look neat and tidy and compact. The Burgundy Rubber has the smallest leaves and is the best choice under 5 feet.

5. **Hawaiian Holly**
   Leea coccinea

   After the **Leea** has been away from the nursery for 6 months, the leaves start to grow in a rounded dome. Only in bright window light does it continue to grow straight up, with leaves from top to bottom. It is cheerful, pretty, undemanding, and easy to care for in any light.

6. **Bottle Palm**
   Beaucarnea recurvata

   Five foot plants are sometimes difficult to get, but they are a show-stopper! No other hardy tropical even comes close to the volume of narrow leaves for the size of the plant. The best plants have the largest base and at least six separate heads.

7. **Selloum**
   Philodendron selloum

   The huge spreading leaves of this plant somehow hold themselves aloft on long stalks. They seem to defy gravity. A single plant can be 8' across at 5' in height. In good window light, a 5' plant may have 50 leaves or more at one time.

8. **Agave**
   Agave species

   The large Agaves grow wide like the Selloum, except that the new spikes point straight up. The heavy leaves are indestructible. A five foot in diameter plant weighs over 100 lbs. They are the best specimen plant for a high light Cactus and Succulent garden.

9. **Areca Palm**
   Chrysalidocarpus lutescens

   Although the Areca is difficult to keep in nursery condition, 5' plants in a 10 inch pot are produced by the growers as a delightful mass of gracefully arching leaves. The 5' Areca is probably the most frequently chosen 10 inch plant at the retail level. It truly is beautiful initially.

10. **Boston Fern**
    Nephrolepis exaltata
    'Bostoniensis'

    After 18 months in light above 100 footcandles (bright artificial), a 10 inch Boston Fern will grow 5' long fronds. When the Ferns are left in the same position without moving them, they become extraordinarily eye-catching. Some Bostons will grow fronds 8' or longer.

Striking 7 Foot Commercial Plants

The appeal of seven foot plants.

Seven foot plants are taller than humans and nothing will disguise their height. Some people may even find this size threatening, so the plant may as well be as aggressive as possible. A 7' plant has been in the nursery long enough to mature completely, and the combination of maturity and overwhelming size are to the designer's benefit.

Tropical plants of this height will always focus attention, just like a table plant also draws a close look. Each specimen must have at least one overriding visual strength. It can be a sturdy trunk, a striking leaf coloration, a great overall size, or large exotic leaves. Whichever appeal the plant has, it will help it be more acceptable to the viewer. A shapeless mass of foliage 7' tall often looks artificial, but a well-formed plant will share its character with those who admire it.

Transporting large plants to the job site.

Plants this size, although mature, pose a few extra problems for the designer. They must be transported with care. Doorways and elevators are just barely large enough. If they are installed when an office is already occupied, the projecting foliage can disturb people and small objects alike. To minimize transportation problems, all large plants should be sleeved until they are in their final location. This protects the foliage as well as the decor.

The major difference between 7' and 5' plants.

Choosing the hardiest plants by comparing foliage texture.

The designer will also notice that 7' plants are the dividing line—where nursery standardization starts to blur. Small plants are produced in less than 1 year, so most are nearly identical—regardless of the grower. Larger plants take more time (1-3 years), and the differences in shading, soil mixes and variety selection have a greater effect on their indoor performance. The best 7' plants have the least coarse foliage—for their type. Coarseness indicates higher light and higher feeding levels. The designer, with a little practice, can select the best plants by comparing a 7 footer to a 5 footer—of the same species. The 7' plant should be just slightly coarser.

10 WINNERS FOR BIG INTERIOR SPACES

1. Kentia Palm
   Kentia belmoreana and forsterana

   Kentias level off at 6 to 7 feet indoors, then start to spread out. The fronds are huge for so small a plant. Kentias have small roots, and a plant will grow to 7' from a 4 footer while staying in the same 10 inch pot. It may take five years until the plant levels off.

2. Lady Palm
   Rhapis excelsa

   Close up, the 7' **Rhapis** is huge and hulking—like a football lineman. But, from a distance, the finely structured leaves give more the impression of a ballerina. This plant has lots of life, and a single specimen can dominate an entire room.

3. Schefflera
   Brassaia actinophylla

   A seven foot Schefflera, grown in a 14 inch tub, turns into a giant after two years indoors. It is one of the few plants that is able to keep a ball shape—even in overhead lighting. Plants this size tolerate 60 footcandles easily—without becoming sparse.

4. Massangeana
   Dracaena fragrans massangeana

   A Massangeana in a 14 inch nursery planter usually starts off four or five feet tall, but even in low artificial light (30 fc), they reach seven feet within two and a half years. The new leaves grow to be five feet long—making the plant's circumference nearly match its height.

5. Marginata
   Dracaena marginata

   There is something breathtaking about the towering, well-formed foliage cluster of a seven to eight foot Marginata. It is so graceful and delicate, it appears to be swaying in the wind. 'Marginatas with Character' are usually produced at this height.

6. Fiddle Leaf Fig
   Ficus lyrata

   It takes a **lyrata** of this size to grow a 4' long leaf. After several years indoors, the stems add several feet in length, and start to bend toward the floor. It is best to let this plant ramble without pruning—to get the most out of its elaborate indoor growth.

7. Bamboo Palm
   Chamaedorea erumpens

   Fourteen inch tubs of multiple Bamboo canes gradually angle away from the planter, to form a perfect inverted cone. This plant grows strongly to 10-12 feet, even in low light, before the foliage gets too heavy for the slender canes. **C. seifrizii** has narrow leaves.

8. Yucca
   Yucca elephantipes

   Like the Cane Massangeana, large cane-type Yuccas impress the observer with their huge straight stems. The tuft of leaves on top are an incongruous finishing to such a powerful start. The larger the canes are, the better the plant looks.

9. Buddhist Pine
   Podocarpus macrophyllus

   The Buddhist Pine, like the Norfolk, doesn't look like much until it reaches at least seven feet. Then the branches sweep dramatically. **Podocarpus Nagi** has coarser foliage and grows more upright—and is a better choice in cool locations.

10. Dieffenbachia
    Dieffenbachia varieties

    A seven foot Dieffenbachia is prized for its giant striking leaves. Even though good window light (at least 300 footcandles) is needed to keep large plants in good condition, they can tower over a small planter garden with an umbrella of color.

Large Specimen Tropical Plants

Plants that are 10' and larger are definitely the most exciting and most challenging assignment for the plant designer's bag of tricks. Large plants have had the time to develop their own distinctive style. No two of them are identical. Each of them makes a significant demand on space and light.

Large plants need extra lighting.

As a rule of thumb, a 10' plant needs twice as much light indoors as a 5' plant. This need for additional light plays havoc with design, since lighting is a people convenience, rarely a plant convenience. A large plant, attempting to survive in less than minimum light, can disintegrate very fast. Fig Trees may completely defoliate in 4 to 6 weeks.

One reason that large tropicals need more light indoors is because growers are forced by economics to produce them in high light—often outdoors—until they have reached full size. Then they bring them in under shade, and wait until the roots and leaves stabilize.

Planting into porous soil is economical in the long term.

A large plant should actually be transplanted into porous soil as soon as it is moved indoors, however, this is rarely done. Some of the better local nurseries—who also specialize in interior landscaping—transplant newly-arrived plants as a matter of economics. They have learned that a well-grown nursery plant takes less maintenance and has a longer indoor life expectancy.

The industry standard replacement rate.

The maintenance industry standard has long been to budget for a 10% annual replacement rate for the foliage plants. However, there is really no reason to expect a plant to fail indoors—unless it is improperly potted, gets inadequate light, or is poorly maintained.

Overwatering often results from poor preparation.

The blame is usually placed squarely on the shoulders of the maintenance personnel. It has often been suggested that poor watering results in 90% of all plant failures. Still, when a plant has been hastily prepared at the nursery (particularly large plants), it may not have much of a chance in any case. The growers and designers must try harder to give commercial maintenance more breathing room in their work.

10 GIANT-SIZE PLANTS FOR COMMON AREAS

1. Fig Tree
   Ficus benjamina

   A large Fig Tree has so many uses, it has become the most frequently specified, big tropical plant. But although a heavy, thick trunk has also become a part of its mystique, a large trunk also means poor low light tolerance. For light less than 150 fc, choose small caliber trunks for any chance of success.

2. Alexander Palm
   Ptychosperma elegans

   This plant only starts to shine indoors when it reaches 10 feet. Then, the contrast between the smooth, strong trunk and the thick, glossy foliage, makes it the most dramatic of the indoor Palms. From a distance, it looks as if the Kentia Palm's fronds were attached to the top of the Queen Palm's trunk.

3. Bottle Palm
   Beaucarnea recurvata

   Although a rarity, the 10' Bottle Palm is truly one of the wonders of the plant world. They are easy to maintain, although the designer should provide considerable light (over 200 fc), or the new growth becomes stunted after 18 to 24 months. Large plants may never need repotting.

4. Fishtail Palm
   Caryota urens & mitis

   Between 10 and 20 feet, the Fishtail boasts the largest cubic volume in relation to cost. Indeed, their spread often equals their height. And, even when grown in fairly high nursery light, the foliage retains a delicate, fresh appearance. They also 'ship' better than most Palms.

5. Tree Fern
   Cibotium schiedei

   Since Tree Ferns are difficult to care for at any height, the large ones, at least, are so feathery and dramatic, they will be widely admired by everyone. In less than 400 fc and 60% humidity, they will need greenhouse rotation every six months to keep them vigorous.

6. Norfolk Pine
   Araucaria excelsa

   The Norfolk is another plant which doesn't really 'mature' until it gets large. On this plant, maturity brings a new shape to the foliage structure. Especially when grown under a skylight, the branches droop attractively under the weight of the needles—but the tips curl upward toward the light.

7. Reflexa
   Dracaena reflexa

   Small Reflexas are bushy and densely leaved. Large plants must be severely pruned, or the slender branches will break because of the heavy foliage. Plants up to 20' are produced like Fig Trees—with a stout trunk sprouting branches clad with leaves. From a distance they are remarkably similar.

8. Areca Palm
   Chrysalidocarpus lutescens

   A 10'-12' Areca Palm is quite unlike a 5' plant. Where the smaller plant is fragile and has soft foliage, the larger specimen has grown a root system extensive enough to support leathery fronds. They are not as durable as the Kentia Palm's fronds—but are more numerous and considerably more delicate.

9. False Aralia
   Dizygotheca elegantissima

   The False Aralia is 5 times easier to keep when 10' tall, than when 3' tall. Like the Areca Palm, its roots need time to mature, before they can adequately support the foliage. In addition, the 10' plants have bigger, heavier leaves, not nearly as susceptible to over and underwatering.

10. Rubber Tree
    Ficus elastica 'Decora'

    The Rubber Tree is magnificient when over 16' tall, but looks less like clusters of oversize leaves on truncated stems when less than 10' tall. At this size, the nurseries prune them like other standard Tree-form plants—to produce a thick trunk which supports a compact foliage ball.

Challenging Plants for Enthusiasts

Some plants are difficult to water. They conspire to make even seasoned maintenance veterans pay attention. When these plants are used at their minimum light, the plus/minus factor in watering is less than 10%. Additionally, they may reward even small mistakes by shedding half their leaves.

Low light watering is the most difficult.

These plants are perfect for those who like a challenge. Low light watering is the most exacting maintenance science. It is the last barrier a plant expert will cross. The satisfactions are great, however, since to grow a beautifully delicate plant—in impossibly low light—will astound all the plant person's peers.

Low humidity compounds the problem.

The most challenging plants have the greatest need for high humidity. To grow them in low humidity means watering at precisely the 'Point of Wilting'. To grow them in low light as well, means watering just a small portion of the central soil mass.

The best technique for watering tricky plants.

A high humidity plant fails in low light, because it never uses water fast enough. Even when watered lightly and sparingly, the soil mass stays wet, and the leaves fall off. The trick is to water just the soil in the centre of the root mass—under the stems. Eventually, the plant will shed the roots at the edges of the pot and grow new ones in the center. After a while, the dry soil around the edges helps to pull moisture away from the central roots—drying them out faster and satisfying the plant's demand for frequent watering, but quickly-drying soil.

This method's advantage over clay pots.

This method for watering is superior even to the drying abilities of a clay pot. Clay pots are excellent for drying the soil out fast, but unfortunately the roots tend to grow at the sides. Thus the central soil in the pot still stays wet while the roots are drying at the sides. It takes a fair amount of practice and nerve to learn to water only the interior roots. But the advantage is the smallest possible root mass, in the easiest to reach location.

THE 10 HARDEST PLANTS TO CARE FOR

1. False Aralia
   Dizygotheca elegantissima

   This is usually the last plant a commercial maintenance person learns how to care for. In bright light it prefers to be almost evenly moist, while in low light it dries nearly half way down before a very sparing watering. Plants over six feet are easier to care for.

2. Ming Tree
   Polyscias fruticosa

   The Ming takes water like the False Aralia, however, the leaves show dryness by drooping before they turn yellow. Both plants shed suddenly from being too wet. Hot air drafts will cause extensive shedding within 24 hours. Small plants (under 2') are the easiest to care for.

3. Citrus
   Citrus varieties

   The Citrus looks so much like the Fig Tree, there is a tendency to water it the same. However, the leaves are thicker and the roots need far less water—poured more sparingly. The various Citrus varieties also require more light than Fig Trees. Table size plants are easier than floor plants.

4. Croton
   Codiaeum varieties

   The Croton is watered like the Citrus, but falls apart faster. The heavy leaves shed quickly from too wet, too dry, and pests. When the Croton is grown in bright window light, care is much easier. A better indoor plant is obtained by growing a small plant into a big one, rather than starting large.

5. Staghorn Fern
   Platycerium species

   Although it looks better mounted on a wall, this Fern is easier to maintain in a pot. Rooted on a slab of bark, it gets trickier, because the slab has to be soaked frequently and thoroughly. In both applications, the leaves droop noticeably before turning yellow. Large specimens get very heavy.

6. Azalea
   Azalea indica

   Unless the Azalea is pinched back regularly and watered perfectly (like the Citrus), it loses all interior leaves and ends up with a few tufts at the ends of the branches. Azaleas will flower once or twice a year when fed biweekly. Always prune immediately after flowering.

7. Maidenhair Fern
   Adiantum species

   This plant is nearly impossible outside a terrarium, unless a watering bucket is kept close by. Large 10 inch plants, especially, can dry out once a day in the summer. However, when well kept, it grows fast. It needs frequent doses of organic plant food to stay green.

8. African Mask
   Alocasia species

   Here is another unforgiving plant—that collapses when too wet or too dry. It is best kept standing on a pebble tray near a sunny window. The first 6 months away from the nursery are critical. After that, the leaves and roots both adapt to lower humidity.

9. Creeping Fig
   Ficus pumila

   Even though this is the sturdiest of Vines, it can turn completely crisp and brown from one day to the next. In the summer, a window plant may need water every two days; in the winter, it stops growing during overcast periods and requires only 1/10 as much water.

10. Table Ferns
    Pteris species

    Table ferns are relatively easy to water, since they like to be kept on the dry side. The challenge with them, is the years it takes to turn a small plant in a 6 inch pot, into a monster in a 10 inch pot. Several different varieties together improve the appearance.

Botannical Name Index

Abutilon striatum–Flowering Maple
    For dependable flowering   13
    For its bright colors   23
Acalypha wilkesiana macafeana–Copper Plant
    For its bright colors   23
Adiantum species–Maidenhair Fern
    For its delicate foliage   25
Aeonium species–Desert Rose
    As a centerpiece   37
Aeschynanthus lobbianus–Lipstick Plant
    For dependable flowering   13
    In hot conditions   33
    In cool locations   35
Agave species–Century Plant
    For its dramatic leaves   21
    Tolerance to chlorine   31
    In hot conditions   33
    In cool locations   35
Aglaonema species–Chinese Evergreen
    In low light   9
    As a shrub   39
Alocasia species–African Mask
    As a challenge   47
Araucaria heterophylla–Norfolk Pine
    In cool locations   35
    As a specimen plant   45
Arecastrum romanosoffianum–Queen Palm
    For its outstanding trunk   27
Asparagus d. 'Meyers'–bottle Brush Fern
    As a centerpiece   37
Asparagus d. 'Sprengeri'–Asparagus Fern
    As a sturdy vine   11
    For dependable flowering   13
    In confined spaces   15
    For its delicate foliage   25
    In cool locations   35
Asparagus retrofractus–Ming Fern
    As a sturdy vine   11
    For its delicate foliage   25
Aspidistra eliator–Cast Iron Plant
    In low light   9
    For physical durability   29
    Tolerance to chlorine   31
    In hot conditions   33
    In cool locations   35
    As a shrub   39
Asplenium bulbiferum–Mother Fern
    For its delicate foliage   25
Asplenium nidus–Bird's nest Fern
    As a centerpiece   37
Azalea indica–Azalea
    As a challenge   47
Beaucarnea recurvata–Bottle Palm
    For its outstanding trunk   27
    Tolerance to chlorine   31
    In hot locations   33
    As a centerpiece   37
    As a 5' plant   41
    As a specimen plant   45
Begonia species–Begonias
    For its bright colors   23
Brassaia actinophylla–Umbrella Tree
    For its rich green color   19
    For its dramatic leaves   21
    As a 7' plant   43
Bromeliaceae genera–Bromeliads
    For dependable flowers   13
    For its bright colors   23
    Tolerance to chlorine   31
    As a centerpiece   37
Calathea makoyana–Peacock Plant
    For its bright colors   23
Caryota urens & mitis–Fishtail Palm
    As a specimen plant   45
Cereus 'peruvianus'–Peruvian Cactus
    In hot conditions   33
    In cool locations   35
    As a 5' plant   41
Chamaecereus silvestri–Peanut Cactus
    As a groundcover   17
Chamaedorea elegans–Parlour Palm
    In low light   9
    For dependable flowering   13
    As a shrub   39
Chamaedorea erumpens–Bamboo Palm
    In low light   9
    For dependable flowering   13
    In confined spaces   15
    As a 7' plant   43
Chamaerops humilis–European Fan Palm
    For physical durability   29
    In hot conditions   33
    As a shrub   39
Chlorophytum comosum–Spider Plant
    As a sturdy vine   17
    For dependable flowering   13
Chrysalidocarpus lutescens–Areca Palm
    As a 5' plant   41
    As a specimen plant   45
Cibotium schiedei–Mexican Tree Fern
    As a specimen plant   45
Cissus antarctica–Kangaroo Vine
    As a sturdy vine   11
Cissus rhombifolia–Grape Ivy
    As a sturdy vine   11
Cissus r. 'Danica'–Danish Ivy
    As a sturdy vine   11
Citrus limon 'Meyeri'–Meyer Lemon
    As a challenge   47

Citrus mitis–Calamondin Orange
    As a challenge 47
Clerodendrum thomsonae–Bleeding Heart Vine
    As a sturdy vine 11
    For dependable flowering 13
Clivia miniata–Kafir Lily
    For physical durability 29
    Tolerance to chlorine 31
    As a shrub 39
Codiaeum species–Croton
    For its bright colors 23
    As a challenge 47
Coffea arabica–Coffee Tree
    For its rich green color 19
Coleus species–Flame Nettle
    For its bright colors 23
Crassula agentea–Jade Plant
    For its outstanding trunk 27
    As a shrub 39
Cryptanthus species–Earth Star
    For its bright colors 23
Cycas revoluta–Sago Palm
    For physical durability 29
    As a shrub 39
Cyrtomium falcatum–Holly Fern
    For its rich green color 19
    For physical durability 29
Dieffenbachia species–Dumb Cane
    For its dramatic leaves 21
    As a 7' plant 43
Dizygotheca elegantissima–False Aralia
    For its dramatic leaves 21
    For its delicate foliage 25
    As a specimen plant 45
    As a challenge 47
Dracaena d. 'Janet Craig'–Green Corn Plant
    In low light 9
    In confined spaces 15
    For its rich green color 19
Dracaena d. 'Warneckei'–Grey Corn Plant
    In low light 9
    In confined spaces 15
    Tolerance to chlorine 31
Dracaena f. massangeana–Corn Plant (bush)
    In low light 9
    For its dramatic leaves 21
    For its outstanding stems
    As a 7' plant 43
Dracaena f. massangeana–Corn Plant (cane)
    In confined spaces 15
    For its outstanding canes 27
    As a 5' plant 41
Dracaena marginata–Dragon Tree
    In low light 9
    In confined spaces 15
    For its delicate foliage 25
    For its exotic stems 27
    As a 7' plant 43
Dracaena m. 'Tricolor'–Rainbow Tree
    For its bright colors 23
Dracaena reflexa–Reflexa
    In cool locations 35
    As a specimen plant 45
Echinocactus grusonii–Golden Barrel
    In hot locations 33
    In cool locations 35
Epiphyllum species–Orchid Cactus
    For dependable flowering 13
Epipremnum aureum–Devil's Ivy
    In low light 9
    As a sturdy vine 11
    As a groundcover 17
Episcia cupreata–Chocolate Soldier
    For its unusual colors 23
Euphorbia splendens–Crown of Thorns
    For dependable flowering 13
    For its exotic stems 27
Ferocactus species–Barrel Cactus
    In low light 9
    In hot conditions 33
    In cool locations 35
Ficus benjamina–Fig Tree
    For physical durability 29
    In hot conditions 33
    As a specimen plant 45
Ficus elastica 'Decora'–Rubber Tree
    For its rich green color 19
    For its dramatic leaves 21
    For its outstanding stems 27
    Tolerance to chlorine 31
    In cool locations 35
    As a 5' plant 41
    As a specimen plant 45
Ficus lyrata–Fiddle Leaf Fig
    For its dramatic leaves 21
    As a 7' plant 43
Ficus retusa–Indian Laurel
    In confined spaces 15
    For its rich green color 19
    For its attractive trunk 23
Ficus pumila–Creeping Fig
    As a sturdy vine 11
    As a groundcover 17
    For physical durability 29
    As a challenge 47
Grevillea robusta–Silk Oak
    For its delicate foliage 25

Hedera canariensis–Algerian Ivy
    As a sturdy vine 11
Hedera c. 'Variegata'–Marengo Ivy
    As a sturdy vine 11
Hedera helix–English Ivy
    As a sturdy vine 11
    As a groundcover 17
    For physical durability 29
    In cool locations 35
Howea forsterana–Paradise Palm
    For its rich green color 19
    As a 7' plant 43
Hoya carnosa–Wax Plant
    As a sturdy vine 11
    As a groundcover 17
    For its bright colors 23
Leea coccinea–Hawaiian Holly
    For physical durability 29
    Tolerance to chlorine 31
    As a 5' plant 41
Livistona chinensis–Chinese Fan Palm
    For physical durability 29
    In hot conditions 33
    In cool locations 35
    As a shrub 39
Maranta leuconeura–Prayer Plant
    As a sturdy vine 11
    As a groundcover 17
    For its vivid colors 23
Monstera deliciosa–Split Leaf
    In confined spaces 15
    For its dramatic leaves 21
Nephrolepis e. 'Bostoniensis'–Boston Fern
    As a sturdy vine 11
    For its delicate foliage 25
    As a 5' plant 41
Nephrolepis e. 'rooseveltii'–Roosevelt Fern
    As a sturdy vine 11
    For its delicate foliage 25
Pandanus utilis & veitchii–Screw Pine
    In cool locations 35
Philodendron oxycardium–Heartleaf Philo.
    In low light 9
    As a sturdy vine 11
Philodendron selloum–Tree Philodendron
    For its dramatic leaves 21
    For its outstanding trunk 27
    In hot conditions 33
    As a 5' plant 41
Phoenix roebelenii–Pygmy Date Palm
    For its delicate foliage 25
    For its outstanding trunk 27
    As a shrub 39
Pittosporum tobira–Australian Laurel
    In cool locations 35
Platycerium species–Staghorn Fern
    For its dramatic leaves 21
    In cool locations 35

Podocarpus macrophyllus–Buddhist Pine
    In confined spaces 15
    For its delicate foliage 25
    As a 7' plant 43
Polyscias fruticosa–Ming Tree
    For its delicate foliage 25
    As a challenge 47
Pteris species–Table Fern
    As a challenge 47
Ptychosperma elegans–Alexander Palm
    As a specimen plant 45
Rhapis excelsa–Lady Palm
    In low light 9
    For physical durability 29
    As a 7' plant 43
Rumohra adiantiformis–Leather Fern
    In low light 9
    For physical durability 29
    As a centerpiece 37
Saintpaulia species–African Violet
    For dependable flowering 13
Sansevieria trifasciata–Snake Plant
    In low light 9
    For physical durability 29
    Tolerance to chlorine 31
    In hot conditions 33
    As a centerpiece 37
    As a shrub 39
Schlumbergera bridgesii–Christmas Cactus
    For dependable flowering 13
Senecio mikaniodes–German Ivy
    As a groundcover 17
Schefflera arboricola–Hawaiian Schefflera
    For its rich green color 19
    As a shrub 39
Spathiphyllum 'Mauna Loa'–White Flag
    For dependable flowering 13
    For its rich green color 19
    As a 5' plant 41
Spathiphyllum wallisii–Peace Lily
    For dependable flowering 13
    For its rich green color 19
    For physical durability 29
    As a centerpiece 37
Syngonium podophyllum–Arrowhead Vine
    In low light 9
    As a sturdy vine 11
Tradescantia species–Wandering Jew
    As a groundcover 17
Yucca elephantipes–Spanish Bayonet
    In confined spaces 15
    For its outstanding canes 27
    For physical durability 29
    Tolerance to chlorine 31
    In hot conditions 33
    As a 7' plant 43

Design Notes:

Order Form

Check Selections

QTY		TOTAL
#1___	**How to SELL MORE Plants** 206 pages w/disk, $59.95	$_____
#2___	**Maintenance Techniques for Interior Plants** 60 pages, 1-10 copies $11.95 11-25 $9; 25+ $7	$_____
#3___	**How to Market Your Horticultural Services** 100 pages, $39.95	$_____
#4___	**Get the Job & Make a Profit** 48 pages w/cassette, $29.95	$_____
#5___	**How to Start Your Own Interior Landscape Business** 36 pages, $9.95	$_____
#6___	**Employee Mgmt Techniques & Personnel Policy Manual** 272 pages w/disk $94.95	$_____
#7___	**Tropical Plant Design** 52 pages, $29.95	$_____
#8___	**The ABC's of Indoor Ficus** 48 pages, $11.95	$_____
#9___	**The ABC's of Indoor Palms** 36 pages, $9.95	$_____
#10___	**Light & Water, Plant Design Basics** 24 pages, $5.95	$_____
#11___	**Indoor Watering Techniques** 36 pages, $9.95	$_____

Book subtotal $_____
CA 7.25% tax $_____
S & H $___5.00___
Total Order $_____

Orders over $250, subtract 15% discount

❏ My check is enclosed

❏ Charge my VISA/MC/Discover/AMEX:

#_____

Expiration Date _____
Signature_____

Please Print

Name_____

Company_____

Address_____

City_____

State, Zip_____

Thank you for your order. Please mail this form and your payment to:
Park Place Publications
P.O. Box 829
Pacific Grove, CA 93950-0829

FOR OFFICE USE:
AUTH#:_____
SHIPPED:_____
OTHER:_____

Money-Back Guarantee
If you are not completely satisfied with any book, send it back for a full refund.

Call Toll free 1-888-702-4500 to Order   www.parkplace-publications.com